I Want That!

I Want That!

HOW WE ALL BECAME SHOPPERS

THOMAS HINE

■ HarperCollins*Publishers*

HarperCollins books may be purchased for educational, business, or sales promotional use. For information, please write: Special Markets Department, HarperCollins Publishers Inc., 10 East 53rd Street, New York, NY 10022.

FIRST EDITION

Designed by Elliott Beard

Printed on acid-free paper

Library of Congress Cataloging-in-Publication Data

Hine, Thomas.
  I want that! : how we all become shoppers / Thomas Hine.
    p. cm.
  Includes bibliographical references and index.
  ISBN 0-06-018511-2
    1. Consumers—History.   2. Consumption (Economics)—History.
  3. Shopping—History.   4. Retail trade—History.   I. Title.

HC79.C6 H56 2002
339.4'7'09—dc21

2002020641

02 03 04 05 06 ❖ /RRD 10 9 8 7 6 5 4 3 2 1

For Beth,
a shopping companion
who always made me see new things

CONTENTS

INTRODUCTION
What Makes People Shop?   ix

1 POWER
**Why We Want Objects
and How They Change Us**   1

2 RESPONSIBILITY
Why Women Take Shopping Seriously   21

3 DISCOVERY
In the Market Among Strangers   41

4 SELF-EXPRESSION
The Blossoming of the Buyosphere   63

5 INSECURITY
Fashion and the Quest For a Great Buy   87

6 ATTENTION
Sellers, Buyers, and the Worlds They Make   111

7 BELONGING
Taste, Lifestyle, and Buying to Fit In   141

8 CELEBRATION
Spending Christmas with Family   167

9 CONVENIENCE
**Efficiency, Branding,
and the Tangled Lives of Shoppers**   185

AFTERWORD
The Future of Shopping   205

Note on Sources and Further Reading   209
Photograph Sources   215
Index   216

INTRODUCTION
What Makes People Shop?

$\mathcal{S}$hopping, I have found, is a subject that makes people nervous. When the subject comes up, they giggle uneasily, as if something deeply intimate and vaguely illicit has come to the surface. In a sense, that's not surprising. Shopping is at once an exploration of desires and a fulfillment of responsibility. It elicits guilt and pride. It can be burdensome or joyous. Our shopping tells us things about ourselves we might prefer not to know.

Indeed, shopping has a lot in common with sex: Just about everybody does it. Some people brag about how well they do it. Some keep it a secret. Most people worry, at least a little, about whether they do it right. And both sex and shopping provide ample opportunities to make really foolish choices. Some shopping is, like sex, an effort to fulfill fundamental biological needs. But shopping, like sex, is often playful, though the play is very serious. In sexual relationships we learn about ourselves in relationship to another person. In shopping, we define ourselves through our relationships to things and to the meanings that our society attributes to them. We try things on, and as we do so, we try on identities. A generation ago, salesladies used to clinch a sale by telling the shopper, "That's you!" Today, we browse through the glossy fashion magazines and rummage through the bargain bins and look, as if into a lover's eyes, and wonder, "Is that me?"

Unlike sex, shopping hasn't been around forever. Some say it's only about two hundred years old, though I put the age at closer to five hundred, which is still but a blip in the million years or so of human evolution. Yet, the acquisition and use of objects, while not unique to our species, is one of our defining characteristics. It is primordial.

It used to be thought that adapting objects as tools is uniquely human, though we now know that's not true. Nevertheless, *Homo sapiens* is the only species that knows it needs something to wear. In the Bible, this insight comes at the same moment as the knowledge of mortality, pain, sex, and the loss of Eden. Part of the terrible knowledge that Adam and Eve gained was that they would need to labor, and still always desire something more.

Shopping is the contemporary expression of our complex relationship to things. Objects are useful. They are repositories of magic. They carry meanings that are more powerful than words because they can embody the paradoxes of life.

For most of human existence, only a few people have had the power to possess large numbers of objects, to manipulate the world, to create images for themselves and their families that the world would recognize. For the billions who live in today's world of abundant consumer goods, this power is commonplace magic. But it is magic nevertheless, and few are willing to give up the power of choosing and owning desirable objects.

Shopping is not inherently good or bad, but it is deeply human. It is the way in which contemporary people address perennial questions: What will we feed our families? How will they be clothed? What tools are needed to survive and prosper? How should we present ourselves to the world? How should we express our deepest beliefs?

All of these questions concern the duties and obligations that tie people together as families and as societies. But within this framework of responsibility, there is plenty of room for choice. Shopping is not the most exalted expression of human freedom. It is, rather, a commonplace freedom that is valuable precisely because it can be exercised every day. This sense of always available possibility is what makes shopping a modern phenomenon. At some times in humanity's past, people may have seen themselves as buffeted by forces beyond their control. At other times, we thought we played a fixed role in an orderly universe. Today, we embrace the dream of self-creation, in an environment of constant flux. We need things to help us survive and prevail in this changing world. We buy them at Wal-Mart, online, at flea markets, supermarkets, Sears, and Saks.

Like other deeply human acts, shopping has some bad aspects. We expend time and money buying goods we might be better off without. We let the incessant dissatisfaction of shopping distract us from pursuits that could be more rewarding. We frequently allow our lives to be measured only in terms of the material possessions we amass. The thrill of immediate gratification can distract us from planning and saving for the future. We participate in a culture of wastefulness that may shadow the lives of generations yet to come.

Yet, despite these psychological quandaries and moral dilemmas, just about everybody shops. It is the aspect of modern living that people in newly developing areas embrace first and most enthusiastically. There are millions of people on earth who live in circumstances where they cannot shop, but most of them would do so if they could. Shopping offers great satisfactions, most of which have little to do with the accusations of self-indulgence to which shoppers are often subjected.

People giggle at shopping, perhaps, because of the absurdity of humanity's fate—looking for a bargain in an indifferent universe. Shopping is ridiculous because what our spirits need is so vastly out of proportion to the goods we settle for. Like the prizes bestowed by the Wizard of Oz, the treasures we cart home don't begin to satisfy the longings that sent us on our journeys.

Several years ago, at a flea market, I purchased a mail-order catalogue from the mid-1950s. Its pulsating pastel illustrations of swooping, jet-age products had caught my eye, but this dog-eared volume proved more profound than I had expected. It offered a view of the passions that come into play when people shop. It offered insights on fantasy and necessity, generosity and greed, thrift and indulgence, identity and possibility. It was an expression of freedom, responsibility, and love.

Someone else had long since pored over these pages, annotating them, ever so faintly, in pencil. Throughout the catalogue, which offered items for every setting from the barn to the boudoir, items had been earmarked for particular people. The handwriting was girlish, but the choices seemed well considered. There were enough erasures throughout the book to indicate that the girl was giving her selections at least a second thought.

The sheer number of contemplated purchases—close to 150—suggested that her generosity was vicarious. But that made it no less real. Surely, she would have bought all these products if she could have, and felt good about bestowing them on each of her carefully selected recipients. She was doing what we all try to do when choosing a gift: connecting a person and the feelings we have toward that person with an item that, in some way, completes, transforms, or at least pleases the recipient.

In some cases, the gifts selected met a practical need. This seemed particularly true of the items marked for Papa: work boots, rugged trousers, a warm coat, a selection of tools. These seemed to suggest that her father lived a life of hard physical labor, probably on a farm. The most grimly useful product selected, however, was probably the new sump pump chosen for Uncle Al.

More often though, the gifts she marked seemed to reflect a desire to transform the recipients by giving them things that they would never buy for themselves. The elaborate slips and brassieres earmarked for Ma, Agnes, and Aunt Lucille probably fell into that category. There were also a lot of pretty clothes reserved for a young girl named Jane, and as I leafed through the catalogue, I began to think that Jane herself was the annotator of this volume. The exercise of being generous to others often leads us to be even more generous to ourselves.

Like many gift-givers, the girl with the catalogue—Jane?— seemed to want to leaven necessity with a touch of luxury. Among the other items earmarked for Ma were an electric range, a steam iron, a supply of pink plastic clothespins, a fine leather handbag, and a dinner dress with sequins. (What would Papa wear when she wore that?)

Even the flannel shirt chosen for Uncle Al in the then-fashionable coral-and-charcoal color combination indicates that his niece wanted him to have something nice to wear. He was more than just a wet basement to her.

The catalogue told Jane about the moment in which she was living. It showed her what colors were new, what appliances people wanted, and what girls her age were wearing, at least in the Midwestern, small-town world reflected in the catalogue. Its compilers were guided by an understanding of what its recipients would really buy. And because people more often buy in order to fit in with their neighbors rather than to compete with them, the catalogue provided Jane and others like her with a guide to belonging in her time and place. In contemporary jargon, the catalogue helped create a virtual community.

As she paged through the catalogue, Jane learned not only about the world, but also about herself. The catalogue contained dozens of dresses and skirts and blouses she might covet, but she selected only a couple of each. In doing so, she was in effect, defining her identity, refining the image of Jane that she presented both to herself and to the world.

A century and more ago, when mail-order catalogues afforded those who lived outside of the big cities their only convenient glimpse of a growing new world of consumer goods, people began to call them dream books. Now, though the dream books have gone, we have almost infinite dream worlds available on the Internet, and huge but cozy communities of consumers accessible through television home-shopping networks. "Just looking" constitutes much of the traffic on the World Wide Web, as it does in the malls and on Main Street.

Still, it's wrong to equate "just looking" with "just dreaming," even if an afternoon at Home Depot or an evening of QVC viewing consists of looking at things that will never be bought. "Just looking" may be more properly understood as a form of domestic due diligence. It is a process of acquiring information, making comparisons, and forming judgments about how to best make use of the resources available.

If this young woman's scrutiny of the catalogue were simply an exercise in vicarious greed, the items she chose would consist solely of pretty things for herself and would, therefore, be far less interesting. What made the annotations fascinating was Jane's effort to be responsible by balancing needs and desires. Being a good consumer is an important part of being a grown-up in contemporary society, especially for women. In another time, Jane might have been expected to learn to spin or to sew, but by the 1950s, it was most important for her to learn how to shop.

And as she marked up the catalogue, she did what all shoppers do. She defined the needs of several individuals she knew well. She imagined how possessions could make her life, and the lives of people she loved, just a little bit different. She confronted a whole world of material possibilities and made thoughtful choices for each person in her life. Deciding how to make the best use of the resources available is not a trivial act. Your future can depend on it. Marking up the catalogue may have been a pastime on a long rainy afternoon, but it was also practice for an important task she could expect to be doing all her life. Learning to shop is a rite of passage to contemporary adulthood. Making material choices is a privilege, a responsibility, and an essential activity of modern life.

For better and worse, it is impossible today to imagine a world without shopping. We live much of our lives in a realm I call the buyosphere. This is, at once, a set of physical and virtual places and a state of mind. The buyosphere is a series of windows through which we are eager to glimpse all sorts of possibilities.

Our contemporary buyosphere consists of a variety of venues—businesslike districts and arty ones, tourist traps and showrooms for people in the trade. It encompasses shopping malls and "power centers," boutiques and big boxes, department stores, outlets, hypermarkets, flea markets, Web sites. It also includes fashion magazines, television programs, newspaper advertisements, music videos, all of the media that prepare us to be shoppers. The most essential part of the buyosphere, though, consists of us, the shoppers. We come into the buyosphere with a mixture of attitudes and emotions. We are serious and lighthearted, sensitive and greedy, thrifty and competitive. The buyosphere is not a civic space, but it is our chief arena for expression, the place where we learn most about who we are, both as a people and as individuals.

During the last decade, the Internet seemed to promise a revolution in shopping. Billions of dollars in losses later, we realize that many people who sought to reinvent shopping never understood it. Just because nearly everybody does it doesn't mean that it's not complicated.

Like a bee in a field of flowers, the shopper in our selling-saturated world is constantly being stimulated, yet always in danger of exhaustion. The economy cannot afford to allow the shopper to become worn out. We live in a global consumer economy in which prosperity depends on the willingness of shoppers to seek out what's new and exciting and different. A collapse of consumer demand—a shortage of shoppers—prolonged the Great Depression of the 1930s, just as it prevented Japan from climbing out of its economic torpor in the 1990s. Consumer confidence is always at risk. It may appear to be a mighty edifice, but if there's a bad enough shock it can disintegrate in an instant. Often in the past, people have transformed themselves from optimistic spenders to timorous savers in a moment, and then required many years of forgetfulness before they were willing to buy into their aspirations. Shoppers navigate through a universe of possibilities, but the most important and least understood choice they make is whether or not to shop.

When times are good and stores are crowded, we say terrible things about shoppers—that they are superficial, and self-indulgent, and wasteful. And those criticisms are sometimes just. Perhaps that's why people stop shopping when they fear for their future. Shopping is an affirmation that there is a future, and that it will be better than today. When people stop shopping, not only are the results economically ruinous, but the culture is signaling that it doubts its ability to succeed.

This book is about the passions that make people shoppers, and how these impulses have changed the world, from prehistoric times to the age of the Internet. It begins not with buying and selling, but rather with using and desiring, which are still at the heart of contemporary shopping. Its aim is to illuminate what's strange about what seems familiar, to seek out the unlikely origins of the routine, and to elucidate the complexity of the apparently simple. The focus is not on the retailer or the marketer. Rather, it is an exploration of the evolving experiences, desires, needs, and anxieties of the shopper.

While it is obvious that shopping is an economically significant activity, it is equally interesting, and less understood, as a part of all our lives. Some call it the world's most popular leisure activity, though much of it really isn't leisure at all. Most people in developed societies spend large percentages of their waking hours shopping, preparing to shop, or being urged to do so. Does all this activity serve to better our lives, or simply to waste our time? My hope is that this book can help us all—as shoppers—to understand ourselves.

The book's approach is to combine an exploration of the passions that animate contemporary shopping with a historical overview of how people understand, desire, and acquire objects. Each of the nine chapters takes as its theme a force that drives shoppers. These are:

> *Power*—the use of objects to assert authority and prove your worth

Responsibility—shopping as a nurturing activity, especially for women

Discovery—going among strangers to trade and learn

Self-Expression—the role of objects in a world where individuals' identities aren't fixed

Insecurity—the conspiracy of shoppers and sellers that conjures the illusion of scarcity and creates fashion to enhance the eventfulness of life

Attention—the craving to have one's desires recognized but not judged

Belonging—the use of objects to forge communities of taste and to rebel against mainstream thinking

Celebration—the ways in which shopping helps give meaning to Christmas

Convenience—the integration and entanglement of shopping with the rest of life

Each of the chapters' themes relates to modern-day shopping, and continues a historical narrative that begins with prehistory and early historical time in chapters 1 and 2, marketplaces in chapter 3, the blossoming of the buyosphere in chapter 4, the development of urban shopping and the evolution of salesmanship in chapters 5 through 7, holiday shopping in chapter 8, and twentieth-century incursions of the buyosphere into every phase of life in chapter 9.

In some ways, this multiple perspective replicates the experience of shopping. The skill of the shopper is, after all, to be broadly attentive. The shopper searches for what is needed, keeps an eye out for what is forgotten, and is open to surprises. I invite you to do the same.

Why We Want Objects
and How They Change Us

I noticed the old woman as soon as I drove into the Wal-Mart parking lot. Actually, I couldn't help it because she was blocking my car. Leaning on her walker, oblivious to the impatient shoppers who were honking to express their displeasure at my refusal to run her over, she made her way, inch by laborious inch, toward the entrance of the sprawling discount store.

She eventually found a shopping cart in the parking lot and, in a quick motion that was almost graceful, picked up her walker and put it into the cart. Then, using the rolling shopping cart for support, she was able to quicken her pace and soon reached the store entrance. And the rest of us were able to park and pursue whatever we were after.

I kept wondering about her as I walked toward the store myself. Why did she feel compelled to go to so much trouble? What did she really need?

Once we were inside the store, our paths kept crossing. Every time I saw her she was at a rack or a bin, closely scrutinizing skirts or shorts or tops. After half an hour or so, she had a variety of small items in her cart, all of them purchases one assumed she could live without, but none of them luxurious or self-indulgent.

When I finally asked her about her trip, she shrugged off the notion that it was an ordeal. She came regularly, by bus, she said. Today she intended to pick up some things she needed around the house and something for her grandchildren, though there wasn't anything she absolutely had to have. "I just like to get out of the house," she said, "and do a little shopping."

What was precious to her was not any particular object but rather the ability to go out on her own and make a choice. She told me that she had to be careful not to put more in her cart than she could carry on the bus. And she needed to be careful with her money. But by getting out to the store, she was able to feel self-reliant, generous, and thrifty. The few items in her cart were almost incidental to her desire to prove something to herself and to those around her. As long as she could get to the store, nobody could say that she was incompetent. She was still able to live a normal life. And by bringing gifts to her grandchildren, she was asserting her importance in the lives of her family members.

You might conclude, then, that the act of going shopping was more important than anything in the cart, but that would not be entirely true. Going shopping might be an assertion of her abilities, but the things she carried home are proof of her power.

Using objects to make connections between people and establish one's authority is an ancient and universal form of human behavior. Other species make limited use of tools to establish specific tasks, but only humans—so far as we can tell—place objects at the very heart of their societies. For all people, at least since Neolithic times, things have been repositories of power. Those who possessed key objects have been the rulers and wizards of their peoples. A king's crown, a chief's mantle, a shaman's collection of mysterious charms, a rapper's jewel-studded teeth have served as sources of authority and magic.

Through most of history, desirable objects have been few and precious. Ambitious people gained dominance by seizing them. Already powerful people maintained their position by bestowing gifts on allies and potential adversaries. Priests and priestesses proclaimed their access to the spiritual world by using ritual objects that invoke supernatural powers. When powerful things fall into the wrong hands, the order of the society is at risk. Throughout history, rulers and religious leaders have worked not merely to amass powerful things for themselves, but to prevent others from doing so. By limiting the dissemination of objects, they sought to keep control.

Contemporary society represents the worst nightmares of such rulers and shamans. Even the poor can afford to live cluttered lives, and amid such abundance it is difficult to establish authority. Possessions no longer affirm the chief's right to rule, but they are essential to the exercise of another sort of power: the consumer's right to choose. My Wal-Mart acquaintance didn't imagine that the items in her cart had anything in common with a monarch's crown, but they were political statements, albeit of another sort. They were declarations of independence.

Even today, shopping is not the only way in which people deal with the power of things. People still steal things, often to seize the power of the things themselves. Young people die because robbers want their cool shoes. And the exchange of gifts is still a very powerful way in which people establish connections and obligations among themselves.

But shopping is our chief exercise of the power of things. It is a ritual so tightly integrated into the fabric of our lives we scarcely realize that it is there. In contemporary society, most people are already learning to shop before they can read a word or utter more than a handful of meaningful sounds. It is, child psychologists have observed, one of the earliest ways in which people begin to understand the world and to develop their personalities.

Three out of four American babies visit a store, usually a supermarket, by the age of six months, though some start virtually at birth. They soon begin to realize that the store is the source of some of the good things that they had previously associated solely with their parents. Some time after that, at around age two on average, they begin pointing at and indicating their desire for things that they see at the store. Most quickly realize that they have a good chance of getting their way. Soon after that, they begin to remember things that they have seen before, or that they particularly like, and asking for them even though they are not in plain view. It is at this point that children become of interest to marketers.

Most three-year-olds remember the layout of the supermarkets and discount stores to which they have been taken, and they often like to be allowed to walk around such self-service places and make selections for themselves. This act of choosing is the most important part of the shopping experience. It starts when children are able to walk confidently, and ends when old people aren't able to walk at all.

Children understand that shopping is not simply about taking, but also about paying. American parents allow their children to select and give the payment for some purchases by the age of five and a half, and allow them to shop independently with their own money by the age of eight.

We all begin our lives as consumers, depending on what others can provide for us. The ability to choose things at a store may not make us truly independent. But it helps us to feel independent, to have that sense of autonomy that is particularly prized by our culture. Moreover, the brightly packaged items that a child sees in the store are treasures. Children play with cans and boxes. They are a spur to imagination, and children often ascribe to them private meanings very different from what marketers intend.

Young people learn to shop just as ducks learn to swim. It's a response both to the world in which they find themselves, and to strengths and characteristics of the species itself. We may not be, as the T-shirt proclaims, "born to shop." But we were born to use objects, and we are raised to believe that selecting them is an important part of being a competent, successful human being. Shopping is so essential a part of our upbringing that it really is a part of how we think and behave. But in order to gain perspective on the power things have in our lives, we must try to imagine life before there was shopping.

$\mathcal{P}$owers of the crown—things make the king

For most of humanity's past, artifacts tell us just about all we know about how people thought and behaved. People were using a very elaborate language of objects thousands of years before there was written language. They acquired natural objects they found precious. They learned how to weave cloth and fiber in designs that expressed perceptions about their society, their environment, and the universe. They learned how to make ceramics that served as vessels for liquids and for meaning. They learned how to hammer out metals to make objects that were gleaming and smooth, and then to smelt the metal to make alloys that were strong and enduring.

People went to great trouble to get the things they considered precious. Many of the valuable Neolithic items that archeologists unearth are found hundreds of miles from either the source of the raw materials from which they were made or from those who likely crafted them. Amber—petrified wood resin—was highly prized as long as ten thousand years ago for ornaments, medicine, and, when burned, perfume. Amber that originated on the shores of the Baltic Sea made its way, in quantity, all the way to the shores of the Mediterranean, evidence of a supply chain that spanned a continent.

Early humans had to struggle for their survival. Few could escape the risk of starving to death. They lived in harsh, unforgiving environments. They had to elude predators. Knowing this, we tend to assume that nearly all human manipulation of the material world was instrumental, even technological in nature. Thus, in hindsight, we view the emergence of metalworking, for example, from the point of view of the superior tools and weapons that could be fashioned from the newly discovered metals and alloys.

During the last two decades, some anthropologists tried to escape this utilitarian economic bias and look more carefully at the artifacts themselves. High concentrations of objects have usually been interpreted as an indication that their possessors had wealth and power. This may be true, Colin Renfrew has argued, but isn't it possible that the concentration of objects is the cause, rather than the result of this condition? We can't be sure, he said, whether certain people possessed things because they were powerful, or whether they were powerful because they possessed things.

And the value of the objects themselves seems not to have come from their immediate usefulness, but from their beauty and from the magical properties that were attributed to them. Finds in the Balkans and elsewhere suggest that the use of metal to create tools and weapons came long after the use of the same metals to make jewelry and other objects that impressed with their sparkle and texture. The development of metallurgical technology eventually helped humans come up with tools that revolutionized their lives and helped them survive. Before that, though, this new knowledge helped people produce things that were thrilling.

Many of these beautiful objects probably had a religious function. Early humans might well have felt that an object that evoked the crop-growing spirits would be more essential to survival than, perhaps, a better hoe. There are many ways for a thing to be useful.

Even some items that appear practical at first glance, such as stone axes excavated at some four-thousand-year-old sites in Britain, turn out to have been finely crafted from materials that made them impractical as tools or weapons, and are preserved in a condition that indicates they were never used. They were Neolithic regalia. It seems likely that the possession of such special things was not simply evidence that some people had attained more power than others. Rather, these luxurious objects were an indication that those who held power did so legitimately. The precious objects were probably not merely a symptom of inequality. They were its justification.

This argument is based largely on the observation of more recent societies. In the African kingdom of Kongo, for example, a leopard-skin robe wasn't merely the mark of the king's position, but an embodiment of power and an affirmation of the legitimacy of his kingship.

The same is true of a monarch's crown. Today we might think of it as a symbol of kingship, or even of nationhood. But it is, even today in most monarchies, a personal possession passed to an heir.

People don't earn the crown on merit, and those who inherit it aren't asked for their résumés. One way of getting the crown is, of course, to seize it. If you are successful in doing so, that has often been taken to mean that the previous ruler didn't deserve the crown, and you do. The crown carries its own power, its own magic. And it finds its way to the right head, or so people like to believe. The king gets the crown because fate, destiny—or God—means for him to have it, regardless of what he might have done to win it.

The Puritans who colonized New England had a similar belief. They saw material prosperity as evidence of God's favor. Thus, while they did not believe in living a self-indulgent life, they viewed those who were able to have fine things as more worthy than those who lacked them, a view many share today.

Seizing things is probably the most ancient means of acquisition. Often, a thief is just a criminal, but sometimes he's a hero. What some anthropologists call nonreciprocal acquisition—robbing, looting, pillaging—have often had higher prestige than buying or trading. When valuables embody the cohesion of a village or a tribe, seizing the treasures of your enemy fulfills two functions. It makes you visibly stronger. And it makes your enemy visibly weaker.

Indeed, a lot of our heroic literature is about someone who is trying to get his hands on a valuable object. Jason sailed after the Golden Fleece. The Arthurian legends recount the quest for the Holy Grail. Wagner's characters and Tolkien's, too, are after a ring. For the hero (as for some shoppers) the struggle of finding is more important than the actual getting. The real story may be that through the process of struggling the hero becomes a hero. But it is still crucial that he is after something and he doesn't go home empty-handed.

Homer's two great epics are set in motion by the seizure not of a thing but of a person. Nevertheless, Homer's characters most often acquire things the old-fashioned way: they steal them. The few merchants that appear in Homer's works, as in so much literature since, are depicted as weak, foreign, and not to be trusted. And while the ancient Greeks often saw the luxurious accoutrements of their enemies as symptoms of weak, feminine character, theft of precious things was thought to be a very manly act.

For millennia, the lure of booty has been one of the main ways in which soldiers have been encouraged to fight. "What a place to loot," exclaimed a German general in 1820, when he first glimpsed London's Regent Street, the most beautiful and opulent shopping venue of its time. More than half a century after the end of World War II, artworks and precious objects stolen during that war, both by governments and soldiers, are still making headlines. The joy of plunder survives, at least in the way we talk about shopping. "It's a steal," says the bargain-hunter who finds an irresistible price.

And, of course, people do steal, availing themselves of the "five-finger discount." According to some retail-industry estimates, as many as one out of eleven Americans shoplift in any given year, and annual losses exceed $10 billion. About a quarter of shoplifters are described as teenage thrill-seekers, and a small percentage of the rest are kleptomaniacs, who have a psychological compulsion to steal, or professional thieves, who plan carefully to steal things they can resell.

Most other shoplifters are very much like other shoppers. They take what they desire rather than what they feel they need. They don't plan carefully. (One particularly hapless case was a woman arrested in Long Island for shoplifting while naked from the waist up. This both attracted attention and made it difficult to hide her pelf.)

Many chronic shoplifters are at least somewhat depressed, and they hope that by treating themselves to new things, they can make their lives seem a bit more complete. Throughout the economic boom of the late 1990s, shoplifting showed a steady, precipitous decline, some of which was attributed to better security systems. Mostly, though, the decline reflected prosperity, as more people were able to pay for what they wanted. Shoplifting, then, is shopping by other means—a way for people to surround themselves with all they think they deserve.

Giving and receiving: Creating obligations, forging alliances

The making of gifts is a far more ancient activity than shopping. It is found in every society that has ever been known, and there is no way to know when it began. Most cultures have developed very complex rituals of gift-giving and exchange. Indeed, some anthropologists have argued that economic life based on money and impersonal exchange is a recent and far-from-universal phenomenon. Giving and taking, they say, are the dominant way in which societies promote cohesion and distribute wealth.

As any Christmas shopper knows, gifts can be sources of enormous anxiety. Gifts embody a relationship. They often create an obligation, or fulfill one. Bestowing a gift is a gesture of respect, and if you do it wrong, you will insult the recipient and invite reprisals. If you make a mistake while sacrificing a gift to the gods, the result will likely be disastrous.

To this day, the only respectable way to receive certain valuables is as a gift. For example, despite recent advertisements encouraging unmarried women to purchase diamond rings and jewelry for themselves, in our culture these are treasures that women expect to receive as gifts from men. A diamond engagement ring is an affirmation of a man's intent to marry and, at least until recently, to financially support the woman. Other gifts of diamonds are displays of devotion or of aggressive extravagance intended to be noticed by others.

As this one familiar example demonstrates, gift-giving is complex. It cements social relationships, mostly by imposing an obligation on the recipient. And what the giver expects in return can sometimes seem disproportionate to the gift. In purely economic terms, a lifetime of keeping house, raising children, and being sexually faithful to only one man is too much to trade for a diamond ring. The point, of course, is that the diamond ring isn't a payment; it's the symbol of a couple's public commitment. But the expense of the diamond ring is important, too. Such serious commitments should not be too easy to make.

Gift-giving creates complicated social networks based on whether one expects a gift, the value of the gift expected, and whether the gift-giving is reciprocal or one-sided. Calibrating and judging the propriety of your gift-giving triggers anxiety. It's a concrete expression of a relationship. And if you've judged either the recipient or your relationship to the recipient incorrectly, it's particularly painful. Unlike an ill-considered remark, which people can decide to forget, the wrong gift endures.

Giving gifts is only rarely an outpouring of generosity or affection. Most are coerced, in one way or another. This is particularly true of the kind of valuable gifts that traveled such long distances in prehistoric times. Many of these were, perhaps, exacted as tribute by powerful rulers from less powerful neighbors. Others were gestures of conciliation, or perhaps shared respect. Sometimes this sort of gift becomes so ritualized that it generates its own sort of object—one used only for gifts.

The most celebrated example of this are the *kula* valuables exchanged by the powerful men of the Trobriand Islands off the east coast of New Guinea. These ornamental items cannot be traded for anything useful within the society itself; restricted to a powerful class, they can only be exchanged within that sphere. By giving them away, one creates obligations and forges alliances that can greatly increase the power of the donor. As with most gift-giving, the thought that matters is the calculation of what one will obtain in return. In some sense, every gift is a Trojan horse.

The menace of luxury

Possession of valuable objects has long been an outward sign of authority, if not its very basis. The regalia makes the chief, and if anyone else tries to amass chiefly things, he is a force for disorder.

The distinction between luxury and necessity that has been part of our thinking from ancient times to the present depends on this worldview. It sees society as static, with a limited supply of material possessions and an agreed-upon center of authority. People are born into a predetermined place in society, and their happiness, and that of the entire society, depends on their knowing their place and fulfilling the role they were meant to play.

Paradoxically, given the aggressive materialism of our civilization, Western thought has long been hostile to the power of objects. The biblical Hebrews set up an opposition between the word, through which the one true God spoke, and the shiny idols that spoke of devotion to false gods.

Meanwhile, the Greek philosophers, and the Romans after them, made a strong distinction between the necessities of life and the luxuries, which they associated with the foreign and the feminine. Indulgence in luxuries, the argument goes, dissipates the energies of a people and leaves them vulnerable to military defeat. This was a warning that was repeated over and over again because it had to be. Luxury is very seductive.

Plato in ancient Athens, and Confucius in China, were products of very different cultures. Still, both were concerned, above all, with a society that was well ordered. In such a society, both argued, the great majority of people should have no more than they absolutely needed to live. To allow large numbers of people to have possessions would dissipate the wealth of the society. Moreover, those who have too much might get an improper sense of their own power and importance that might lead them to challenge—or even ignore—authority. Yet, necessity is a very slippery concept. No society has ever been found in which everyone subsisted at a level of pure animal sufficiency; Plato and Confucius lived in powerful, prosperous places where nearly everyone had more than the minimum required to live. In effect, both proposed an ideal of simple dignity, of having enough but not too much, and not wanting more. They envisioned societies in which each person would occupy a clearly defined station in life, surrounded by the objects appropriate to his or her role. People would be satisfied to have what others like them had, but no more.

For centuries, luxury was seen as a form of weakness, bordering on sin. The most influential Roman writers disapproved of luxury, and celebrated masculine, martial values. Echoes of their disap-proval can be heard nearly two thousand years later in the popular view that the luxury and decadence led to the fall of the Roman Empire. Self-indulgent ways of living are believed to have created an opening for the virile, uncorrupted barbarian hordes to take over. The Romans spoke of the Persians as self-destructively luxurious. We say the same of the Romans, and worry vaguely about our-selves.

Luxury was seen, as Communism later was, as an enemy within, capable of hollowing out a society by undermining the values and understandings that hold it together. The spread of luxury was, in fact, understood as a redistribution of wealth in the society away from common interests, as money was spent for private pleasures rather than common needs. One of its greatest dangers was that those who adopted luxurious ways of life would abandon their roles as artisans, farmers, merchants, or soldiers.

If too much consumption by the wrong people was a peril to people in power, then it stands to reason that the elite would fight back. They did so, at many places and times, in the form of sump-tuary laws. These were regulations that dictated what members of particular classes were expected to own and wear, and frequently identified things they were forbidden to own or wear. (School uni-forms, justified as ways to preserve order in schools and to keep young people from wearing inappropriate clothing, are a classic contemporary example of sumptuary regulation.) Sumptuary laws tend to be revised frequently, and they are very specific about the things that are forbidden. They offer a reliable record of fashion throughout history because it seems that, at any given time, there are very popular objects and styles to which right-thinking people object. In recent years, for example, the sport-utility vehicle has been singled out as a symbol of inappropriate consumption, a pri-vate indulgence that threatens the general welfare. Calls to regulate SUVs out of existence have had little impact, but even if it hap-pened, sumptuary laws are rarely effective. There's always a new fashion, a new outrage, coming along.

Neither Plato nor Confucius, brilliant as they were, could have conceived of such a thing as Wal-Mart. And it's very unlikely that they would judge its contents to be necessities. They would see anarchy, a society whose members don't know their place and things are utterly out of control.

Even we—the barbarians at the checkout counter—continue to share some of their unease about luxury. To be sure, we often use "luxury" as a word of praise, to indicate something we consider highly desirable. Owning a luxury car, for example, is good if you can afford to do so. Even so, mixed feelings remain. We justify indulgence in luxury as a well-deserved reward for hard work. The company president who drives a luxury car is to be admired. The welfare mother who drives one is a symptom that the social order is askew. Seeking the flashy and opulent simply for its own sake is highly suspect. We are bothered by people who have become too rich too young because we believe that they have not fully earned the lavish lives they are able to lead. We fear that too much wealth can lead you astray. During the stock-market boom of the 1990s, many affluent parents attended expensive seminars on how to prevent their children from becoming spoiled brats.

While we speak about luxuries and necessities as if their meanings were self-evident, it is difficult to make a real distinction between them. Often, it seems that our definition of a luxury is something we don't buy for ourselves. Sometimes, though, it's something that we don't believe that people less worthy than we are deserve—the porterhouse steak paid for with food stamps, for instance.

Standards change over time. Everyone would probably agree that, in the modern world, lightbulbs are an absolute necessity, though until a bit more than a century ago, even a king or a robber baron had to get by without them. Obviously, food is a necessity, but the various processed and prepared products that take up most of the floor space at the supermarket cost many times as much as their raw ingredients. We are accustomed to paying for the convenience of not having to actually prepare food. This is arguably a luxury, but people who work long hours and feel they don't have time to cook find convenience foods a necessity. Clothing is obviously a necessity, but how full does your closet have to be before your wardrobe crosses the line from necessity to luxury?

If one could look objectively at the array of stuff available at Wal-Mart—and I'm not sure that's possible—one might conclude that there is hardly anything on sale there that a person couldn't live without. You don't absolutely require a lawn sprinkler. You don't *need* Barbie. You do need water, but you don't need bottled water. Nobody needs a ceramic sculpture of mother and daughter hippopotamuses, but at under eight dollars, few would label it a luxury.

Many of the products we find at Wal-Mart—even such familiar items as gloves and stockings and tailored trousers—were once very luxurious products. But modern production and distribution methods have made them inexpensive, unexciting, and universal. None of the tens of thousands of objects manufactured throughout the world and available at Wal-Mart is, by itself, all that important. Still, all have some meaning, at least at the moment we buy them. The goods still offer a residual sense of accomplishment and enrichment, though it fades away quickly.

The great majority of the offerings at Wal-Mart and similar mainstream, low-price retailers are goods that may be inessential, but which become necessities once you have decided to live in a certain way. Although we sometimes assume that people consume in order to compete with one another, more often than not, we consume to belong. We want to have what those around us have. These object then become defined as our necessities. Once you buy the house with the lawn, you realize that you need to get along with your neighbors. While a verdant lawn might, or might not, fill you with joy, a parched, brown lawn certainly will draw disapproval. You buy the sprinkler and it feels like a necessity. Whether you knew it or not, you made the decision to buy the sprinkler back when you decided to buy the house, and even earlier, when you decided to live in a free-standing house rather than in an apartment or townhouse.

If I came into your house and declared "You have too much

stuff," it's very likely that you would agree with me. If, however, I started ridding your house of things I deem to be unnecessary, before very long we'd be arguing. "Who are you to judge what I need or don't need?" you'd ask. "Why should you be entitled to dictate what items I should have?"

Nearly everyone would agree with you, because we live in a society that, with very minor exceptions, treats consumption choices as a private matter, almost a sacred one. You have the right to have what you choose, provided that it doesn't overtly endanger others. Nobody has the authority to tell you otherwise. Your home is your castle, and you have a right to your own regalia. An attack on your stuff is an attack on your sovereignty.

*A*lways wanting more

Throughout most of history, few people had more than a couple of possessions, and as a consequence, people were very aware of each object. Life was austere. The ability to be bored by a material surfeit was a rare privilege. There are many stories of kings and emperors who sought a simpler life, if only briefly. Now, that emotion has become widespread, and those who wish to simplify are identified as a distinct market segment. Whole lines of "authentic" products have been created to serve this market, and magazines are published to tell people what they need to buy to achieve a simpler life. In our age of careless abundance, austerity is a luxury, available only to multimillionaires, the occasional monk, and the really smart shopper.

"The standard of life is determined not so much by what a man has to enjoy, as by the rapidity with which he tires of any one pleasure," wrote Simon Patten, the pioneering economist-philosopher of consumption, in 1889. "To have a high standard of life means to enjoy a pleasure intensely and tire of it quickly." Patten's definition of the standard of life was based on superfluity: He expected that people would always have more than they need and would never have all they might want. That was a novel idea in Patten's time, and it is one that still makes many people uneasy. In material terms, it seems terribly wasteful, a misuse of the resources of a finite world. And in psychological terms, it seems to trap us in a cycle of false hope and inevitable disappointment. We work in order to consume, and we consume in order to somehow compensate for the emptiness of our lives, including our work. Indeed, there is some evidence that people who feel least fulfilled by their work are the most avid shoppers, while those who love their work find shopping a burden, though they don't necessarily buy less.

Our materialism is oddly abstract, a path toward an ideal. The things we acquire are less important than the act of acquiring, the freedom to choose, and the ability to forget what we have and to keep on choosing. We don't aspire, as people in China did during the 1970s, to "Four Musts": a bicycle, a radio, a watch, and a sewing machine. We aspire instead to such intangibles as comfort and modernity, qualities for which standards change so rapidly that the buying can never stop. "Progress is our most important product," Ronald Reagan used to say during his tenure as spokesman for General Electric. And in 1989, after the Berlin Wall fell, multitudes throughout Eastern Europe disappointed intellectuals in the West by behaving as if freedom was the same thing as going shopping. Even China moved on in the 1980s to the "Eight Bigs": a color television, an electric fan, a refrigerator, an audio system, camera, a motorcycle, a furniture suite, and a washing machine. Now China is moving beyond the specific "Bigs" and aspires to more, a quest that will never end. Wal-Mart is opening stores there.

It is amazing to think that from the dawn of time until the time of Adam Smith, a bit more than two centuries ago, people believed that wanting and having things was a drain on wealth, rather than one of its sources. That doesn't mean, however, that they didn't want things or that they didn't, at times, go to great lengths to attain them.

Now, as I move, mildly entranced, behind my cart at Wal-Mart, grabbing items I feel for a moment that I need, I am assumed to be increasing the prosperity not merely of my own country, but of the entire world. Indeed, in the wake of the World Trade Center attacks, American were exhorted not to sacrifice, as is usual in wartime, but to consume.

There are those who disagree. Can the massive deficit that the United States runs with other countries, which is driven by our hunger for ever more low-priced goods, be sustained indefinitely? Does our appetite for inexpensive goods from overseas exploit the low-wage workers who make them, or does it give them new opportunities? And more profoundly, are there enough resources in the world to provide everyone with this kind of living standard and still have enough clean air and clean water? How many Wal-Mart shoppers can one planet sustain?

These are serious questions that need to be addressed, but those who raise such issues have rarely considered the power of objects and the fundamental role that acquiring and using objects has played since prehistoric times. In this story, the big box stores, boutiques, malls, Main Streets, Web sites, and other retailers that constitute the buyosphere represent the fulfillment of an ancient dream. The local Wal-Mart is a wonder of the world. Never before have so many goods come together from so many places at such low cost. And never before have so many people been able to buy so many things.

Nevertheless, we yawn at Wal-Mart rather than marvel at it. That such a store could provoke apathy instead of amazement is a perverse tribute to the plenitude of our consumer society and the weakness of the emotional ties that bind us to the many objects in our lives. Never before has so much seemed so dull.

And even if Wal-Mart is not the noblest expression of personal liberty or the highest achievement of democracy, we should consider that it does provide a setting for exercising a kind of freedom that has threatened tyrants and autocrats for thousands of years. Like the old woman with her walker, we go to Wal-Mart to acquire things that prove our own power. It is a place where people really do get to choose.

2
RESPONSIBILITY

Why Women
Take Shopping Seriously

*S*hopping is a highly responsible job. The shopper spends most of the household income, and family members expect to get something in return.

And it is a responsibility that is most often exercised by women. Throughout the world, women are the most serious shoppers. In marketing surveys in North America and Western Europe, the evidence is overwhelming. Women see shopping as an important part of their lives. Men tend to see it as an extraordinary response to some pressing need. In America, women make 73 percent of all trips to the supermarket. This statistic probably understates the percentage of routine purchases they make, because other studies show that men's supermarket trips are often quick emergency runs to pick up a handful of needed items—often using lists compiled by the woman of the house.

As she pushes her cart through the store, the shopper is constantly making judgments. She considers how to spend a limited budget, and balances this against the needs and desires of her family. She worries about whether her children are eating the right foods, and whether her husband is getting too fat. She knows that her children are clamoring for products that their friends have or that are being sold to them on television, and she must make both a financial and an ethical decision about whether their desires should be fulfilled. Each purchase helps constitute the taste and image to which she aspires. By her shopping, she determines what family members will eat, what their home will look and feel like, and, to a large extent, what everyone will wear. She defines the very fabric of her children's experience: what they touch, what they see, what they eat. Her purchases constitute a reality, a morality, and an image for members of the household. This is an immensely powerful role, though the power is very different from the assertive, magical use of objects described in the previous chapter. This kind of power is constrained not simply by limited income and the way in which messages from commercial culture influence her family's desires. The most important constraint is a keen sense of obligation to others. For the shopper, making choices feels like a heavy responsibility.

Shopping is the moment when shared wealth is consumed. It is important not to waste your resources. In traditional societies, wealth often takes the form of livestock that the family has nurtured for years, and its slaughter becomes a ritual event, a time of celebration and anxiety. In the modern world, our labors rarely have any direct connection to what we consume. Yet people still feel anxiety about consuming. It is still important that the fruits of their efforts not be squandered. That's the responsibility of shoppers.

There is a vast literature of marketing surveys that analyze differences in men's and women's shopping habits. Marketers know in great detail the kind of settings women prefer and the kind men prefer. They know, for example, that women want to be able to feel the fabric of a blouse, while men like to feel that their shirts are wrapped and untouched. Their solution to these diverging desires is to add a slit to the wrappers of men's shirts so that women, who buy a substantial minority of them, can feel the fabric.

Since the 1970s, while the impact of feminism has blurred many sex-role differences, women's domination of shopping has not diminished at all. Indeed, it has increased. One reason is that women's incomes have risen, giving them both more power within the household and the ability to live outside of families. Another is that the percentage of men holding mechanical jobs has declined, and with it their authority over purchases of automobiles, hardware, and other traditionally masculine products.

The distinct roles the sexes play in shopping must reflect something important about our culture. They certainly provide a context for understanding the way in which the value and importance of shopping has historically been at least undervalued and often feared by men. But explanations for the sexes' different attitudes toward shopping often degenerate into exercises in pop physiology or anthropology, and they tend to ignore the important ways in which shopping and sex roles have changed over time. A more powerful explanation recognizes that shopping is, much of the time, a way of assuming responsibility.

How women shop; how men fail

Here's what it's like to shop like a man.

Yet another vacuum cleaner had died, and I'd been advised it would be cheaper to replace it than repair it. I had driven to a suburban "power center," to shop at a "big box" appliance store.

So there I was, facing about two dozen upright vacuum cleaners. Their price tags ran from just over $50 to just under $500. Each was carefully designed for its market and price point, but they all looked the same to me.

I could see that the cheaper ones had cloth bags in ugly colors, the midrange tended to be superaggressive Darth Vader black, while the most expensive affected dark burgundies and rich-looking, sports-car greens. Some had complex filtration systems. Some channeled the dirt into two compartments, while others used bags. Some of them had lights to tell you when you had vacuumed enough, but I had read in *Consumer Reports* that these weren't worth having. I had scribbled down the model numbers of the magazine's recommended vacuum cleaners, but none of these were available.

I faced the selection with profound pessimism. Any choice I made seemed doomed to fail. I felt myself becoming nervous and irrational. I was desperate to pick something, just so I could leave.

I tried to fall back on the numbers, but my high-school physics couldn't provide the answer. Are 12 amps better than 1,000 watts? And how do those compete with 4 horsepower? Almost blindly, I grabbed one marked "Mach 2.7," even though I knew that it didn't travel at nearly three times the speed of sound.

"What does Mach 2.7 mean?" I asked the salesman as he wrote up my purchase.

"The Mach 2.7 is more expensive than the Mach 2.1," he replied, "and not as expensive as the Mach 3.3 or 3.8. It's a good cleaner, though. And you're getting it for a great price." Feeling foolish, frustrated, and a bit angry, I picked up my vacuum cleaner and left.

Later I discovered that those numbers, uninformative as they may be, are put on vacuum cleaners to appeal to male shoppers' attraction to quantity and brute force. Market researchers have determined, the *Washington Post* reported, that what men are looking for is "maximum suck." (In December 1999, Sanyo announced a breakthrough: a cleaner that sucks and blows at the same time. That might be too subtle for us guys.)

I had started out impatient. I arrived underprepared. I felt the store wasn't doing enough to help me find what I need, but I didn't like having to deal with a salesman. Rather than focus on the nuances of the various products, I saw them all as a blur. And that was probably because I felt that buying a vacuum cleaner was something I shouldn't have to do in the first place.

A woman would have done things differently. Buying a vacuum cleaner would not seem an affront; it is something she would expect to do. She wouldn't be embarrassed to know something about vacuum cleaners, and she would try to learn something before she went shopping. In the end, she might well have been susceptible to the same sale price that hooked me, but she wouldn't feel awful about it.

Contemporary women understand their role to be that of Chief Consumption Officer for the household. They grant the men in their households a measure of power over purchasing, but not much. In a 1998 study conducted by Simmons Research, 73 percent of women interviewed said men influence food buying, but only 13 percent called that influence very important. Similarly, nearly half said men influence furniture purchases, but only 12 percent called this influence very important. The only purchases where men were at all decisive was automobiles, and just under half deemed men's judgment very important. Car ads that stress raw power are aimed at men. Those that stress safety, reliability, and getting away from it all are aimed at women.

Women's buying power is strong in areas where you don't really expect it. Home Depot has been remodeling its outlets to change them from glorified lumberyards to comprehensive home decorating centers, reflecting the reality that women are as likely to be remodelers and do-it-yourselfers as men. Women purchase 75 percent of all items featuring logos for National Football League teams. Most are not buying these team jerseys and other items for themselves, but for others.

The point here isn't that men don't like to buy and own things. They certainly do. It's just that they are less likely to enjoy looking for them, comparing items, seeking bargains and values. It's not their job. Men may shop, but it's not what they do.

Two women out of three say that they enjoy shopping, while only one man out of three gives the same answer. Women rate shopping as their third most enjoyable leisure activity, after vacations and dining out, while men rank it last. Men are most satisfied with the clothes they wear if the women in their lives help them pick out those clothes. By contrast, women are most satisfied with their shopping experience if the men in their lives stay home or do something else. The latest things in malls are entertainment attractions that "baby-sit" men while women shop.

One study revealed that if you put men and women on treadmills, the man will walk faster. But if you put the same couple in a mall, the woman will walk faster. Women feel that they are accomplishing something when they shop. Men don't.

Men are not raised to view shopping as a useful activity, much less an achievement. A British researcher has found that some male Christmas shoppers experience stress levels similar to those found in jet fighter pilots and police officers entering dangerous situations.

Moreover, men perceive most of the shopping streets, malls, boutiques, and department stores that make up the buyosphere as women's worlds, filled with perfume smells and a vast array of garments covering a gamut of quality, prices, tastes, sizes, and situations whose nuances men don't understand. It's not by chance that department stores typically locate men's clothing near the door. Recently, some have begun to place them in separate buildings with their own entrances, so that men won't risk encountering the mysterious female spaces that dominate most stores. Women revel in profusion. Men want to grab what they came for and get out.

When it comes to clothes, of course, men have a narrower range of acceptable options. Women have a greater freedom to define an individual style by the way they dress, a freedom that imposes a greater burden of selection and that increases the possibility of making a serious mistake. Because women need to make subtle choices about their wardrobe, they need to work harder at it than men. And that probably explains why the most exasperated shoppers are busy women with highly responsible jobs, many of whom would probably welcome the limited range of choices available to their male counterparts.

Oddly enough, on the Internet, where one can find a particular item with rifle-like precision, sex roles are reversed. Several studies indicate that men treat the Internet more playfully, and spend more time wandering about and entertaining themselves. Women who shop on the Internet do research, then zero in on a product and buy it—online or, more often, in a store—just as men are said to do in the real world.

This role reversal in cyberspace seems to suggest that, at least up till now, men feel more comfortable on the Internet than women do. They feel free to explore what's available on-line, just as women do at the mall, which men perceive as being an increasingly feminine place. As we shall see, the buyosphere—at least' the real-world shops, stores, streets, and centers where most shopping happens— has been directed primarily at women for most of the last two centuries. One might expect that as the roles, training, education, and income of men and women converge, the buyosphere would become more hospitable to men. But that seems unlikely to happen because of a widespread belief held by marketers that men and women are fundamentally different. Besides, women control most of the spending money.

$\mathcal{A}$re women born to shop?

There are two popular, purportedly scientific explanations for the differences between men's and women's shopping behavior. The first says that women's brains are different from men's, and somehow more shopping-oriented. The second argues that most of humanity's past was spent in hunter-gatherer cultures, and women were the chief gatherers. Shopping, then, is seen as the contemporary manifestation of gathering.

These two ideas are complementary; many people believe in both. Each has some facts in its favor, though neither is a truly scientific hypothesis. They give rise to some interesting conjectures that cannot be proven either way. But the hunter-gatherer explanation has become a sort of truism, frequently cited both by marketing professionals and journalists. Thus, these explanations deserve some attention, if only because they are so widely, if superficially, believed.

Women's brains are a bit different, on average, from men's, though neuroscientists who map the brain by measuring its responses to specific stimuli have not yet pinpointed a female-only shopping center in the cerebrum activated by the announcement of a blue-light special. The main way women's brains are different is that they're smaller, averaging about 91 percent the weight and volume of a man's. Men once viewed that as a sign of superiority, but in the age of the computer, women's brains seem superior. They have just as many nerve cells as men's do, but in a smaller package. When two computers have the same amount of processing power, the smaller one has the advantage because it can work more quickly. Most women have a bit more brain, per unit of body weight, than men do.

The other physical difference is that the connections between the two sides of the brain are better developed in women than in men. This is the characteristic that might make the difference. Shopping is about observing a large number of products and making connections between what is available and what is needed or desired. Some speculate that a better-integrated female brain can deal more comfortably with these disparate stimuli than can the more compartmentalized brain of the male. This makes a sort of sense, though there is no research to back it up.

Indeed, the mental capacities of men and women are overwhelmingly similar; we're the same species, after all. There are only a couple of statistically significant differences. One is that men are, in general, better at thinking in three dimensions and mentally rotating objects. This is associated with higher performance in some areas of mathematics. In evolutionary terms, this strength is thought to be related to "circling," the ability of many creatures to move in a consistent circle that will take them back to the point where they began. Men exhibit circling behavior more strongly than women do (though store designs are often shaped, in part, by the well-documented tendency of both men and women to move toward the right once they walk in the door.) Among other primates, male circling behavior is associated with finding females with which to mate. Presumably, males who were able to go far from home and find their way back to safety dispersed their genes more widely and had an evolutionary advantage. Many shopping environments are intentionally disorienting, which is potentially more irritating to those men who take pride in their superior sense of direction. However, a connection between men's spatial perceptions and their behavior as shoppers has not yet been studied, let alone established.

While men are better at going around in circles, women have

the edge in communicating and establishing social relationships. The ability to understand signals both from the environment and from other people and to communicate with your children and make them aware of danger helps more offspring to survive. At least until recently, shopping, too, has been a social occasion, one in which the shopper needed to relate to a large number of merchants, salesclerks, and other shoppers. The shopper needs to take in a large amount of information very quickly, so communication skills are very important.

Yet most men spend their working lives in social situations, and they must also digest information and communicate with others. Historically, they have suffered no disadvantage as workers, only as shoppers. Brain structure and evolutionary neurology can tell us why, on average, boys do better on the math portion of the SATs, while girls do better on the verbal section. It hasn't quite told us, though, why women are more serious shoppers.

But the possibilities suggested by brain structure do seem to dovetail with the pop anthropology explanation for women's prowess as shoppers. Men are inherently hunters, the argument goes, while women are gatherers. As a consequence, men find what they're looking for and buy it, while women shop. This explanation is so easy, and it seems to account for so much, that it sounds too good to be true.

The hunter-gatherer way of life is believed by many to describe all cultures from the time human precursors first arose about a million years ago until they began establishing permanent settlements in Asia, North Africa, and Europe about ten thousand years ago. In this view, civilization is a recent innovation. It was as hunters and gatherers that we became what we are. Moreover, some anthropologists have observed tribal peoples living a life they presume is much the same as that implied by archeological remains from mankind's first nine hundred and ninety millennia.

The hunter-gatherer concept is far more controversial among anthropologists than many lay people recognize. It is, itself, a sort of intellectual compromise in a scholarly battle of the sexes. During the 1950s and early 1960s, anthropology was preoccupied with explaining how the combination of attributes that characterize humans—including walking on two legs, language, tool use, and highly developed brains—first evolved. The dominant line of thinking, summed up in Richard Lee and Irven DeVore's 1968 book *Man the Hunter*, argued that the development of these characteristics was driven by men cooperating to hunt creatures larger than themselves. Women, in this view, were relegated to a passive reproductive and maternal role. Some even suggested that women remained in a four-legged, virtually subhuman state long after the males had begun standing upright.

The concept of the gatherer was a feminist riposte to this theory. Archeological remains disprove any fantasy that early humans were dining nightly on mammoth they had speared that afternoon. Early humans mostly ate plants, supplemented by animal protein from fish and small animals that could be trapped, and from other creatures, termites for instance, that didn't have to be hunted. Recently, archeologists have discovered early evidence of hunting with nets, an activity that typically includes women and children along with men. Nets themselves, along with other kinds of woven products, were seen as the sort of soft female inventions that are undervalued because they are less likely to survive than hard, male-identified artifacts, such as spear points.

There are unwarranted stereotypes embedded in these arguments. Men who fish have often woven their own nets, and there are contemporary peoples whose women make spear points. The hunter-gatherer concept was created to give women a sort of separate but equal status in the making of mankind. But while there is ample evidence that gathering was an important activity among early humans, neither hunting nor gathering was the exclusive province of either sex.

Among contemporary hunter-gatherer peoples, the distinction between the two activities is far from clear-cut. Although caring for children dominates the lives of women in virtually every culture that has been studied, there are examples of women who hunt with bows and arrows, with spears, and with nets. Sometimes they hunt while carrying children on their backs. There are also examples of egalitarian societies in which some men gather tubers, and some women hunt, according to their abilities and inclinations. Now that women run companies, we are able to recognize the aggressive, sometimes violent role played by some of the female members of the Mbuti people of Zaire or the Batek Dé of Malaysia.

Yet it does seem that although women do some of the hunting in some places, among most cultures they still do the majority of the gathering. And being a gatherer, recent research suggests, is not the passive activity that many had assumed it to be. It is very, very difficult.

One group that lives at the edge of the Kalahari Desert in southwestern Africa uses eighty different plant species as food, including various kinds of melons, roots, leaves, tubers, and gums that they gather from a large geographical area. This is a far more varied diet than that of most residents of developed countries. Gatherers must be sharp-eyed to find this diverse but not abundant food. The women go out, often in groups, carrying their tools and nursing infants in a leather sling. (The baby sling is as common among hunter-gatherer peoples as stone axes. Some feminist scholars suggest that it should be recognized as one of humanity's first tools, one that freed many hands to accomplish other things.)

The Kalahari women nurse their children until they are nearly five. The weight of the nursing children, a digging tool for roots and tubers, and a club to kill small animals and birds, along with the foodstuffs and firewood the woman gathers often add up to as much as 75 percent of her body weight. In each of the first two years of her children's lives, it has been estimated, a Kalahari woman will carry them 1,500 miles.

This gatherer's life is a lot harder than a trip to the mall. If she were suddenly thrust into a modern consumer lifestyle, she would view it as being radically different from grueling daily search for sustenance.

Yet there is something familiar about this woman, simultaneously looking for eighty different plants and a few dozen kinds of small animals and insects while taking care of her children even as she seems not to be paying very much attention to them. This ability to attend to many different things simultaneously is essential to being a successful shopper. Indeed, recent studies of women shoppers indicate that having children along cuts the length of a shopping trip only slightly. (Having a man along, though, shortens it a lot.)

Could it be that the structure of the woman's brain, which appears to have more connectedness among its parts than the typical male brain, was shaped by an ancient need to do dozens of things at once while carrying screaming children? If that's really so, then most contemporary shopping environments, which offer thousands of things to be ignored and only a handful of items to be noticed, arguably play to the strengths of the female brain.

These speculations are amusing, but they rest on shaky underpinnings. There is nothing in the structure and physiology of the brain that suggests that females are hard-wired to shop, while the hunter-gatherer hypothesis is an oversimplification that is becoming less useful to anthropologists—if not to marketers—every day. Besides, they suffer from a fundamental flaw: They ignore history. Women haven't always shopped as they do today.

Choosing as nurturing

Perhaps I was more inclined to give credence to the hunter-gatherer explanation because I identified with those children in the slings. My mother was a fierce and voracious shopper. Her enthusiasm for the hunt was not at all dampened by her plight as a widow with two children and a low-paying job who couldn't afford to buy much of what she found. (My mother was, I have discovered, fairly typical of low-income people who deal with their unhappiness by periodically purchasing a luxury.) On Saturdays, my mother would drag me out of the house and into department stores. I would sit, for what seemed like hours, on streamlined modern shelves beneath the racks of dresses while my mother foraged through great piles of stuff, looking for a bargain. I didn't much like doing that, though I find, as an adult, that I'm inclined to be something of a forager and bottom-feeder myself.

But one day when I was talking with my mother about shopping, she shook my inclination to believe in the unbroken continuity between prehistoric gatherers and ourselves. "Your grandmother had to work very hard raising the six of us," she said. "But one thing she never had to do was shop for groceries."

Was she telling me that this activity, which smart people have said was primordial, wasn't even as old as my own grandmother? In a sense, she was.

My mother explained that her mother, living in New Haven, Connecticut, during the first half of the twentieth century, never had to do the kind of concentrated gathering that we see as commonplace. There was a grocery store less than a block down the street, which granted credit to its customers. She had six children. One of them was usually around to be dispatched to the corner to get whatever Grandma needed. And if what the grocer gave her didn't meet Grandma's expectations, she would not hesitate to send the child back to the store to return the unacceptable product. Some days, the children would go to the grocer's half a dozen times.

She could trust her children to shop mostly because there was little shopping involved. One walked up to the counter and asked the grocer for a pound of butter, a pound of coffee, or a chunk of cheddar cheese. The selection consisted of primary ingredients that enabled my grandmother to make what she needed from scratch. The grocer stocked only a few convenience products in which these ingredients were combined or processed into crackers or pancake mix. Mostly, the grocer offered a handful of basic commodities.

Today's ever-expanding supermarkets offer tens of thousands of branded products, each of which expresses its own values, its own claim to usefulness, nutrition, cleanliness, or health, its own fantasy. Each product represents a distinct, anxiety-inducing choice. My grandmother would send my mother to the corner to purchase flour, lard, apples, and sugar, and then make a pie. Her modern counterpart can purchase a premade crust, choosing an acceptable fat content, or a whole frozen or fresh-baked pie. She can also pick any one of hundreds of other desserts my grandmother might have liked if she had been given the opportunity to buy them.

My grandmother used the same kind of soap to wash her clothes and her children, and often used the same washtub for both tasks. Today's consumer can choose among dozens of soaps and scores of detergents, fabric softeners, and other products for the laundry. The contemporary shopper needs to ponder how these cleaners will affect her skin and how badly they'll pollute the planet. My grandmother could never have imagined such convenience and choice, but she never had to bear the burden of choosing.

The freedom that my mother envies in her mother's lifestyle is, ironically, a freedom from convenience. Women of my mother's generation were happy not to have to use a washboard, felt liberated by frozen vegetables and delighted by Sara Lee. Unlike the woman of the Kalahari, searching for nutritious roots, laboriously digging them up, dragging them back to the settlement, and pounding them with stones, the contemporary supermarket shopper chooses among conveniences. She may not feel, however, that life is easy. The time all these products save gets eaten up by other tasks and obligations.

What unites my grandmother, the Kalahari gatherer, and the contemporary supermarket shopper is not a propensity to shop. Rather, it is the willingness to take primary responsibility for the material well-being of their families. The Kalahari woman must work to find the food, carry it back, process and prepare it. Women of my grandmother's time didn't have to forage for nutrients. But she did have to labor to process and prepare the food, make, mend, and wash clothes, keep house, and otherwise attend to the nutritional and material needs of her husband and children. The contemporary shopper's chief task is the challenge of choosing among things that have already been processed. Still, the goal of seeing that the family is fed and the household is maintained remains much the same.

$\mathcal{P}$riestesses with shopping carts

The argument that I've been advancing—that shopping is a modern way of assuming a primal responsibility—seems at odds with the most common stereotypes of shopping. Our popular culture tells us that shopping is an orgy of irresponsibility in which improvident housewives run amok in the aisles spending money they don't have. It also tells us that shopping is, at its purest and most exquisite, an undisciplined rampage of selfish consumption. After all, the word most commonly paired with "shopping" is "spree."

Spending one's wealth always creates anxiety. This became especially true during the nineteenth century as agricultural and artisan households—in which all the family worked and consumed together—were replaced by households in which men earned money outside of the house, and women stayed home and spent it. The man bankrupted by the profligate ways of his self-indulgent wife became a familiar object of pity and ridicule, whether or not such a plight was actually as prevalent as the jokes and newspaper stories suggested.

The other stereotype, that of orgiastic waste, contains within it a desire for transcendence. People always hope that the fruits of their labors more than meet their needs and provide them with an escape from the routines of life. Yet, although people do occasionally splurge when they get a sudden windfall or when they go on vacation, shopping is most often one of the routines of life. It doesn't offer an escape. Store owners urge shoppers to loosen their inhibitions, but most of the time, people shopping are well aware of their responsibilities and constraints. The spree is a sort of fantasy. Day-to-day shopping is different, less exciting, more sustaining.

Over a period of a year in 1994–95, anthropologist Daniel Miller interviewed residents of a mixed-income, mixed-race area of North London both as they shopped and when they got their purchases home. He asked them what they bought, why they bought it, what their purchases meant to others in their households. As he recounted in his 1998 book *A Theory of Shopping*, even they undervalued the difficult task of meeting their daily needs with limited money. They told him that he should be writing about "real" shopping, the free, wild kind. But Miller had a different agenda.

He was trying to understand what real shopping was for most people—that is, for people with limited money who were nonetheless incessantly importuned to buy. These were people who had to work as hard to decide what not to buy as what to choose, and were often disappointed that they couldn't meet everyone's desires and aspirations. He encountered a few flamboyant thieves and some who habitually failed to limit their purchases to their money on hand. But most of the shoppers with whom he spoke were trying to save their money and provide the best value for their families and themselves. Most shoppers liked to give themselves a treat, to compensate for the lack of appreciation from others for their careful choosing. But for most of his informants, there was little hedonism in their shopping.

Having provided a nuanced, realistic view of the shopping experience, Miller's book goes several steps beyond and gives this dullest sort of shopping a cosmic meaning. Shopping does connect with something deep, ancient, and widespread in human behavior, he argues. But the shopper isn't a descendent of Stone Age gatherers. Rather, she is more like a priestess. And shopping is a ritual of sacrifice.

The ceremonial slaying of a goat and burning of its entrails doesn't seem to have much in common with a trip to the ShopRite. But Miller observes that in most sacrificial cultures, there are countless small and routine sacrifices that are still considered to be essential to the cosmic order. When the rituals of sacrifice aren't observed properly, disaster often follows. By definition, sacrifices involve consumption, but they are also intended to ensure that the things sacrificed will not go to waste.

"The premise of shopping, like that of sacrifice," Miller writes, "is that it is the precise moment when everything that had focused upon the accumulation of resources is about to turn into the moment when those same resources are expended. . . . Sacrifice ensures that the very best of what society has produced is effectively and efficiently spent to obtain not merely mundane provisioning but the benefits of a relationship of love and devotion to a divine force."

A sacrifice, he says, consists of three stages. The first is the moment of expenditure, such as the slaying of the animal, the offering of the fruits. The second stage involves isolating that portion of the sacrifice that is sacred, which belongs to the gods. In several cultures, this is done when the entrails are burned and the smoke that rises into the air is viewed as the property of the gods. In Jewish tradition, blood, viewed as life itself, is the sacred portion. In Jewish ritual slaughter, it must be returned to God and not eaten by humans. The third part of the sacrifice is when the sacrifice becomes food, and people eat it.

It's not difficult to see how the first and third aspects of sacrifice are part of daily life, but it's harder to discern the central stage. To what gods are things being sacrificed? And what is the part of it that belongs to the gods?

Based on his interviews, Miller concluded that the central aspect of the shopper's sacrifice is the aspiration to thrift. Virtually every shopper to whom he spoke expressed a belief that shopping must be done carefully so that money won't be wasted. The shopper should look out for sale items, for coupons, or for items that, though they might be more expensive initially, will last longer and offer greater value in the long run. By striving to be thrifty, the shopper tells herself, she is holding back part of what she would ordinarily spend, in order to achieve a more transcendent goal. By economizing, she can tell herself that she is making a sacrifice to ensure the future of her family. She is careful, not wasteful. By observing the rituals of coupons and discount cards, the shopper can reassure herself and demonstrate to others that she takes a sacred responsibility seriously. And the receipt tells her exactly how much she has saved by shopping carefully.

By shifting the focus from the mere act of acquisition to the rituals, procedures, and responsibilities that surround it, Miller provocatively explains why shopping feels so important. Shopping is a ritual, and like all rituals, it must be done properly or something will be lost. You must strive not to pay full price. The discounts you receive are an offering to the future.

One good thing about Miller's theory is that it gives the act of shopping a primordial resonance, while making allowance for the fact that shopping and gender roles have changed over time and will continue to do so. By contrast, to identify women shoppers with prehistoric gatherers is to imply that shopping is somehow instinctive and that women must always be the primary shoppers.

Still, the idea that shopping is somehow a woman's secret seems likely to persist, if only because so many people—many of them women—want to keep it alive.

For most of the last two centuries in industrial societies, many workers have been discouraged from looking to their work as the source of identity and solace. Instead, they have been encouraged to enjoy the fruits of their labors, the goods they can purchase with their wages.

During the same period, women have been given the key role in deciding what will be consumed. Paradoxically, this important economic role seems to be associated with their role as mothers and nurturers, the embodiments of love, devotion, sacrifice, and other values that we believe transcend the world of money, buying, and selling.

Could it be that the job of the shopper—a task that leaves her both unappreciated and deeply satisfied—is really to bring home things that money can't buy?

3
DISCOVERY

*In the Market
Among Strangers*

I n the early spring of 1978, I spent several days at the bazaar in Kāshān, in central Iran. I had been traveling by myself for eight months and had resisted the commercial temptations of some of the great cities of the world. Suddenly, in Kāshān, I was not just in the market, but *in the market*—looking, listening, seeking discoveries. After a long period when my mind had been preoccupied with other matters, I was once again exposing myself to temptation. Once again I was shopping.

It helped, of course, that I was in a very special place in the buyosphere: a Persian bazaar. Wandering through its labyrinth, I could see wool being dyed, carpets being woven, and brass being beaten. I could smell the spices and the pastries, and I couldn't avoid the aggressively ingratiating merchants. The bazaar at Kāshān is a particularly beautiful one, with its mud-covered domes seeming to explode out of the dull, dense, constricted city like bubbles of pure energy. Bazaars can be disorienting, even sinister, but at that moment I was engaged. The bazaar was a spectacle in which I was delighted to be playing a part. It seemed about as far from a routine shopping experience as possible. The exotic setting and goods, the aggressive sociability, the intense bargaining all seemed to add up to "real shopping." And I bought.

Markets and fairs are the oldest and most enduring part of the buyosphere. They are found, in one form or another, everywhere on earth. Nobody knows how long people have come together in a particular spot at a particular time to trade with others. There were markets, some archeologists argue, even before there were cities and towns. And once most people abandoned nomadic lives for settled ones based on agriculture, markets permitted people to trade their surpluses. This increased the efficiency of the land and enabled some people to develop skills that weren't directly related to getting food.

There are markets in Europe that have endured in the same location from the time of the Romans and before. And while markets reflect changing conditions—that is their job—markets from different times and places have much in common. For most who come to them, they are a break from their daily toil. They are highly sociable, but in a superficial way. You deal in the market not as a member of a particular family or clan, but as someone who wants to buy or sell. Transactions there are made at arm's length, without obligations on either side. Though an atmosphere of trust and confidence is essential for the market to work, the focus is on the goods available.

In a market, one usually finds many people selling the same commodity, so it becomes important to compare quality and price. But one can also find items that are unique or new. In an extraordinary circumstance, one might find an original copy of the Declaration of Independence tucked behind an ugly framed print, as once happened at a flea market in Adamstown, Pennsylvania. More likely, you can find a trendy new ingredient for sale at a farmers' market years before it shows up in the supermarket.

For those accustomed to modern shopping, being in a market is both exhilarating and stressful. In Kāshān, I couldn't just wander the bazaar in a self-absorbed and passive state, as I would in a shopping mall back home. One of the pleasures and trials of a traditional market is that one makes connections with the other people there.

You go to the market not just to buy things, but to meet others and to learn things. Yet every market transaction is also a social transaction, involving tea and conversation.

"A young girl went blind making this carpet," says the rug salesman. If true, this claim would be appalling—and most of the women in rural Iran would be blind. In fact, it is merely a bit of salesman's hyperbole, a way of underscoring the fact that making a carpet is hard labor, worthy of a high price. Yet it's the kind of complex, ambiguous, and repellent image that has been filtered out of the experience at, for example, Wal-Mart. If we discover that a pair of their cheap sneakers was made by ten-year-olds in Asian sweatshops, it's shocking, because everything at Wal-Mart seems bland and impersonal. But here in Kāshān, a childs' sacrifice of her health becomes a mark of authenticity, which, the salesman knows, is what foreign tourists are very likely seeking. In the market at Kāshān, I bought some beautiful carpets that I still have in my home. Like most people who have bargained in a bazaar, I suspect I probably paid too much for them.

Rationing scarcity

Historically, markets have rarely operated every day. Within the Roman empire, for example, produce markets were held every eight days; in medieval Europe, every seven days; and at a similar interval in Asia. Nearly all of the week was spent producing things. Only a small amount of time was given over to obtaining consumables one did not produce.

Eight years after Kāshān, I was in another market far from my home, this time in central Colombia. Half a year earlier, a landslide caused by a volcano nearly fifty miles away had, without any warning, buried the town of Armero, including all its buildings and many of its inhabitants in nearly twenty feet of mud. A total of twenty-seven thousand people died in the eruption. (A day or two later, a couple of former residents returned to the disaster site with picks and shovels and robbed the bank.)

When I visited, plans were under way to construct a new town some distance from its old site, presumably out of harm's way. The refugees were still living in temporary huts scarcely larger or stronger than shipping cartons. Many were enraged at the government, the volcano, and each other. There was an undercurrent of violence about the place. The night before, machete-waving townspeople confronted and intimidated a government official who had come to offer an update on the slow progress of the project. But these survivors armed themselves also to protect themselves from their neighbors, whom they darkly accused of conspiracies to profit from the catastrophe.

The morning of the market, though, everything was outwardly peaceful and harmonious. Along the single street of the refugee encampment, people squatted in front of their huts. What they wanted to sell was laid out on the ground in front of them. Just about everyone was selling potatoes, though nobody had more than three or four. A handful had some droopy carrots, a few had onions, and one had five plump tomatoes for which he was asking an enormous price. There were few sales. There was nothing much to buy. Yet most of the people in the village were out on the street, examining the offerings of their neighbors. They talked and gossiped as they went. Despite the tensions in the village, the morning market was an outwardly convivial occasion.

Some might say that what these people were doing wasn't shopping at all because the participants had few financial resources and little to choose. Nevertheless, some of the key aspects of shopping were on display in even this most minimal of settings. The villagers were discovering what was available to them, and also learning what their neighbors had to offer. Whether it's preteens scoping out each other's backpacks, or impoverished villagers judging their neighbors' potatoes, shopping involves assessing one's own status and calibrating one's aspirations. These can happen even if there are no goods to buy, or if you don't have the money to buy them. Shopping involves gathering information about the people with whom you live. It enables you to keep score of your own place in society. It provides an opportunity to be superficially sociable with a wide variety of other people. The market is a place where you present yourself, and where you learn about others.

The feeling of these two "traditional" markets was very different. Most people would probably deem the one in Kāshān, with its sense of abundance and of sensory overload, to be the true market, and the impoverished one in Armero to be an anomalous result of natural disaster. In fact, the bazaar in Kāshān represents an advanced, affluent stage in the development of the market, while the one in Armero, because it was both brief and sparse, comes closer to the way in which most markets throughout history have operated.

Historically, markets and fairs were devices for dealing with a scarcity of goods and of time available to obtain them. Both buyers and sellers benefited from having markets open only briefly and at predictable times. The buyers could be confident that they would not have to interrupt their other work to try to determine when needed goods would be available. The sellers knew that they would be able to offer their goods to the maximum number of buyers, and thus obtain the best possible price. The markets' short duration forced everyone to show up at the same time, which offered opportunities to renew contacts regularly and to gather information. Even today, many antiques markets operate only one day a week, or for a few days each year, in order to assure that the greatest number of buyers and sellers will be present.

The most important characteristic that distinguishes shopping in a market from routine contemporary shopping is that markets consist entirely of personal transactions. One does not deal with some distant manufacturer, represented by a brand, or with chain-store employees who have little personal investment in what they sell. If you go to a market often, you get to know other people there, both merchants and fellow buyers.

The downside of such marketplace society is that human relationships are as likely to impede sales as encourage them. Some merchants are unpleasant; you must decide if their offerings are desirable enough to offset the bad experience of buying from them. And because choosing things is such a big responsibility, it is easy to be put off by a merchant who seems to be passing judgment on your aesthetic taste, nutritional choices, or thriftiness. This is true even though some of the most impersonal kinds of retailers—such as supermarkets and Web sites—are nosier about your consuming habits than anyone in a marketplace could ever be. But one surrenders information to such businesses passively and impersonally, by using a discount card or clicking a mouse. By contrast, a marketplace merchant with just the hint of a smirk can cause you to doubt your judgment and shake your will to buy.

Markets demand a higher level of attention than is required by most modern shopping. This can be fun, but it can also be exhausting, especially in markets, like that in Kāshān where everything needs to be bargained for. While economists love this kind of market because it promotes price efficiency, those who are actually in the business of selling things know that when people have to commit themselves emotionally to each thing they purchase, they will buy less. Nearly every major retail innovation during the last four centuries has attempted to reduce the fatigue and the personal friction of the marketplace.

The dangers of markets

The sociability of markets contrasts so strongly with the impersonality of supermarkets or discount stores that the contemporary shopper cannot help but notice the difference. For those going to markets centuries ago, however, the sensation was different. The market was a place where one could encounter strangers. Markets have often been on the boundaries between two tribes or nations. Even in village markets, one met people who weren't relatives or neighbors. The value of the market was that it offered a window into a wider world. This also posed a certain amount of danger.

Although marketplaces have always existed in some form nearly everywhere, they offer possibilities that have often appeared disruptive to social stability and corrupting to public morals. Contemporary political and economic ideology sees markets as the basis of all economic life; their ubiquity seems to prove the point. Yet markets are only one way in which goods have been exchanged, and they have more often been treated as a necessary evil than as an organizing principle.

One of the earliest descriptions extant of the glories of a great market city is also a powerful condemnation. The Phoenician city of Tyre in what is now Lebanon was, like New York and Hong Kong, a cluster of islands near the mainland, which grew into a great port. For the prophet Ezekiel, writing early in the sixth century B.C.E., it was glorious and vain:

> All the ships of the sea and the sailors in them visited you to trade with you . . . They brought you glory . . . and helped make your beauty perfect . . . People paid you in silver and iron, tin and lead for your merchandise . . . They bartered men and bronze implements. The people of Beth-togarmah traded you horses, chargers, mules . . . You were paid in ivory tusks and ebony. Edom exchanged carbuncles, purple, embroideries, fine linen, coral and rubies against your goods. Judah and the land of Israel also traded with you, supplying you with corn . . . wax, honey, tallow and balm.

The list goes on, including wine, wool, horsecloths, lambs from Arabia, spices, precious stones, and gold from Sheba. But the reason Ezekiel has provided this detailed inventory is as a prelude to his prophecy of its destruction. "Your heart has grown swollen with pride owing to your splendor," Ezekiel's Yahweh tells the city. "By the immense number of your sins, by the dishonesty of your trading, you have defiled your sanctuaries. I have brought fire out to consume you." (The city was destroyed twice, first by the Babylonian king Nebuchadnezzar, a few years after Ezekiel wrote, and finally by Alexander the Great in 323 B.C.E.)

Ezekiel saw such a concentration of goods to be, in itself, corrupting. (Similar feelings that gaudy materialism must ultimately be punished may well have been a motive for the destruction of the

World Trade Center.) For Ezekiel, once riches become too important, wealthy people begin to see themselves as if they are gods. Another less obvious danger comes from the way in which wealth brings so many disparate peoples together. Strangers present temptations; it is easy to be dishonest with people you will never see again. Disapproval of treasures and possessions suffuses the entire Bible; they almost always lead to disunity and discord among a people whose survival was always in doubt. The values of the marketplace challenge ties to one's family, clan, or tribe. Ezekiel prophesied that the people of Israel would be spared from the destruction he foresaw precisely because they identified themselves as one people with one God.

While the ancient Israelites were exceptional among their contemporaries in their declared contempt for material goods, there have, from ancient times to the present, been people who believed that markets undermine virtue. This is a particularly important issue today, especially for parents who seek to protect their children from what strangers are incessantly selling them. Indeed, the conflict between family values and market values is fundamental.

Markets are mechanisms for allocating goods. While they are ancient and widespread, they are not the only means of doing so. In most places at most times, only a small percentage of the society's wealth came to market. Instead, it was allocated by families, clans, tribes, and within feudal relationships that were seen as extensions of family ties.

There is nothing "natural" about markets. After all, a baby doesn't need to go to market to buy milk. Her mother provides it. That's a biological fact that allows the species to survive. The family, an extension of this primal sharing, is based on the notion that the strong share with the weak and those with surpluses share with those facing shortages, in order to promote the survival of all. Having a large family and maintaining close ties with cousins is thus a form of social insurance. And in nearly all societies, these ties are cemented by rituals that involve exchanging gifts among those with close ties. Such an outwardly mutual gesture helps disguise the fact

that the values of the gifts are often unequal and the wealthier sub-
sidize the needier. The expansion of interlocking family obligations
leads to the formation of clans and tribes, larger institutions that
promote the collective welfare, though usually in less personal
ways. In all cases, though, the ultimate goal is stability.

Even when such a group accumulates a substantial surplus,
more often than not its response is not to trade the surplus but to
try to save it. People know that good times don't last forever, and
they want to be provided for in bad times. It may be that politics
begins with storage. One of the most common responsibilities of
being a chief, both in prehistoric and more recent tribal societies, is
that he is the keeper of the community's resources. He sees, for
example, that granaries are built and maintained. Then having
done so, he obtains great power from deciding who should have the
grain and under what circumstances.

In ancient Egypt, markets played a minor role. In their place
was a bureaucracy that managed food production and allocated the
harvest, a system that lasted thousands of years. Throughout the
pre-Roman ancient world, in medieval Europe and Japan, and in
countless other places and times, family-based distribution systems
evolved into feudal arrangements, in which farmers gave up much
of their crops to noblemen, whose responsibility was to protect
their dependents from outside threats. Markets existed to trade the
small amount left over after all obligations were met.

Collective consumption and markets coexist within all complex
societies, even when the prevailing ideology suggests otherwise.
The Roman Empire had no great belief in markets; it sought to
organize and dominate trade. But it created an atmosphere of political stability in which they were able to flourish. Markets are at their
best when people feel confident going among strangers.

Good marketing in Athens

Ancient Athens was one of the most confident and innovative cities
that ever existed, and it is not surprising that one of its distinguish-

ing characteristics was a market that formed the very center of the community. The Greeks were successors to the Phoenicians in their domination of Mediterranean trade. But while Tyre was famous for large-scale trade from around the world, we don't know anything about its retail markets. We have no real sense of whether it was a good place for individuals to buy. Athens unquestionably was.

There, warehouses and wholesaling were concentrated at the port of Piraeus, four miles outside of the city, while, beginning in the sixth century B.C.E., an important retail market was created in the agora in the city's center. This was the result of a conscious decision to clear the land for the market, and keep it clear. The Athenians also built workshops around the periphery of the market from which goods were sold, as well as buildings of public importance. Nobody knows precisely why the Athenians decided to give retailing such a central place, but the historian Herodotus saw it as something that made the Greeks different from the barbarians. In the entire Persian Empire, he said, there wasn't a single marketplace.

From what we know about the agora, it was a place where modern shoppers would feel perfectly at ease. An affluent market, its goal was to organize and celebrate the city's abundance. Each commodity was sold in its own area, so it was possible to make a rapid survey of all the fish, all the live birds, all the fruit and meat that was available each morning. There were stalls selling sheep, and other stalls selling the cloth, leather, and sausage that could be made from them. There were people selling omelets, to be consumed on the spot, and others selling incense, wine, honey—and slaves. (Nearly everywhere there have been markets, humans were among the things bought and sold.)

The agora was primarily a food market, though the places that generated much of the traffic were hairdressers and sellers of perfumes and ointments, establishments where people liked to linger. It was said that every male citizen, and the many slaves who actually did most of the shopping, passed through the agora every day. This makes sense because commercial cities like Athens depended on a flow of information, and in the days before telephones and other communications devices, nearly every such city had a time and a place where everybody met. The merchants of the agora kept short hours; they opened in midmorning and closed shortly after noon. Thus the market was limited to its own part of the day, and nearly everyone in this compact city of about fifty thousand went there around the same time.

The agora is remembered as a public place, a market that generated philosophy. (A ceramic wine cup excavated in the agora is inscribed with the name of a wine seller at whose stall Plato said Socrates liked to drink.) It is celebrated as an ideal civic realm, where public issues were debated.

But it was primarily a commercial place. Aristophanes and other comic playwrights dramatized the passionate yet playful negotiations between cajoling purchasers and merchants who tried to intimidate them, even though they knew their squid was valuable only for a moment. Buyers were warned to beware of the merchant who wet his wool to make it heavier, and not to buy a basket of figs without looking below the top layer to see if those below were equally appealing.

The Athenian agora was a lively, colorful, crowded, well-organized but apparently chaotic place, a close cousin of the bazaar at Kāshān, and of the contemporary affluent markets at Union Square in New York or Pike Place in Seattle. When we read about it, we feel we know it, that we have been there. It seems that all markets have always been the same. And yet, familiar and generic as it seems, the Athenian agora was a rare sort of place, and Europe, at least, would not see its likes again for more than a thousand years.

Making change

The success of the Athens agora can be attributed in no small measure to an invention that had been introduced shortly before: small change. Coins of large value, made of gold, had been around for centuries. The Greeks attributed the invention of coinage to the Lydians, who lived in what is now Turkey, not far from the realm of the legendary King Midas. His dilemma—that all he touched turned to gold, creating a wealth that was useless—had its origin in the problems of real marketplaces. Gold coins were simply too valuable for everyday transactions. In many cases, they were kingly treasures, to be amassed rather than spent. While they could be exchanged for humbler, more necessary items, one gold coin could easily be enough to purchase half a shipload of grain.

Only when silver and copper coins began to be minted did the chief business of ancient marketplaces shift from barter to retail trade. The introduction of low-value usable money tremendously eased and accelerated trade and made markets far more useful. Paradoxically, low-value money, which circulates freely and rapidly, enables the creation of far more wealth than money such as gold coins, whose value is high and incontrovertible. Nowadays, of course, even paper money accounts for only a small percentage of most people's purchases. Money is information stored in a computer and accessed with a plastic card. It is completely insubstantial and thus even more easily spent.

The use of low-value money is such a convenience, and such a spur to retail trade, you might imagine that this was an invention, like the wheel, which once developed, would never be abandoned. This proved not to be the case.

Unlike gold coins, whose value lies in the substance from which they are made, low-value money depends on a general atmosphere of trust and political stability. In such an environment, you can sell to a stranger and feel confident that the money he pays you will be accepted by others. Thus, all sorts of coins circulated throughout the Roman Empire, and they were relatively easy to exchange for one another, though one did pay a fee to do so.

Financial transactions in the ancient world were often closely associated with temples and other religious buildings. Money, like religion, is mysterious and demands belief. Even today, the United States, the nation that pioneered the separation of church and state, prints "In God We Trust" on its currency. (When Jesus threw the moneychangers out of the temple in Jerusalem, he was doing something that most of his contemporaries wouldn't have understood. The moneychangers weren't seen as defiling a holy place. They were exactly where those who needed them expected to find them.)

But once the Roman Empire fell in the west, small change virtually disappeared from circulation because relatively few people were willing to accept it. The general atmosphere of trust was gone. For centuries, ordinary people engaged in very few monetary transactions. They lived within a network of obligations. They paid rent for their land by giving up a percentage of their crops, and also by being willing to fight when their landlord demanded. In return, they received a measure of military protection and stability. Cash rarely came into the equation.

You went to market with the surplus from your share of what you grew, after the landlord took his cut, then bartered it with others. Previously, markets were able to offer a variety of goods, because the availability of cash attracted goods from a longer distance. Barter trade meant less variety and fewer transactions. A lot of the time, the weekly market must have looked like the one I saw in Colombia, where each seller offered nearly identical and equally shriveled produce.

From the eleventh century on, silver coins began to be more common in Western Europe, some of them minted by major markets and ports themselves. Still, their relatively high value got in the way of trade. Basic items like ale and bread were so inexpensive that no coin existed small enough to buy them. People resorted to cutting the existing coins into pieces, though that undermined confidence, because those who cut the coins were likely to keep a sliver of the silver for themselves.

Only when Europe's kings consolidated their power over their realms did things begin to change in the markets. Small coins meant more business, and because the crown was increasingly powerful, more people were willing to accept them. The revival of cash trade set the stage for the great medieval fairs, which were truly international events.

The peace of the fair

Markets move the goods because they don't depend on any tie of family, loyalty, or obligation between buyer and seller. The market itself is a kind of battlefield, as both buyers and sellers seek to charm and intimidate their way to an acceptable price. But in order for these commercial battlefields to prosper, there must be peace, or at least a truce, and a set of rules that all participants accept.

Medieval European markets began with the ringing of a bell, while fairs often began with religious ceremonies dedicated to the patron saint whose feast the fair celebrated. Doing business before the market or fair began was strictly prohibited. Trying to buy goods that were on their way to market, or before the stalls officially opened, was known in England as "forestalling." Because it was a threat to the integrity of the market, it was subject to heavy fines and punishments. A similar and equally serious infraction was what was called "engrossing": purchasing supplies of a similar commodity from many different sellers for resale at a higher price. This practice was later known, of course, as wholesaling, and it became the basis for the retailing system as we know it today. In the medieval market, though, it was a violation and a sin, because it betrayed the expectations of those doing business in the markets.

Only at the market did people have access to standardized weights and measures. Those who cheated at the market were often punished, publicly and immediately, even while the market was going on. Those selling spoiled food were often forced to eat it in the presence of their dissatisfied customers.

During the great fairs, all laws of the locality were suspended and a special, highly restrictive legal code took effect for the duration. There were even courts—in England they were known as courts of "pie powder," a corruption of the French *pieds poudres* or "dusty feet"—that were in session only during the fair and which sought to complete their deliberations and their punishments before the fair ended. Judges of such courts were often merchants at the fair who had been pressed into service. They were often very harsh with their competitors, and always fast. They could not afford to let proceedings drag on, because they feared losing business in their own stalls.

Those who went to the fairs seemed to have accepted the harsh justice and quick penalties, much as shoppers today accept greater restrictions on their behavior in the mall than on the street. Fairs were, after all, dangerous places, filled with strangers. Many who attended them did not handle money regularly. Because they had to carry enough with them to pay for a year's worth of purchases, fairgoers attracted pickpockets and con artists. Entertainers and prostitutes also sought a share of the contents of the purse. All sorts of appetites were aroused in a way that didn't happen during the rest of the year. It was both exciting and frightening.

Even peasants were sometimes able to make their way to the fair. Life on the land broke the back and numbed the mind. One worked incessantly, using tools and methods that had been in use for more than a thousand years. It is difficult for those of us who live in an atmosphere of constant imagery, stimulation, and entertainment to imagine what is was like to live in a world where the most intense aesthetic and sensory experiences were found in church. To walk through the gates of a fair must have been an entry into a different life. There were crowds of people you had never seen before. There were jugglers in bright costumes, and menageries with strange animals. There were merchants selling silk, which must have seemed incredibly luxurious to those who owned only a couple of rough, homespun garments. There were many items that only a handful of the people at the fair could afford. But everyone who came could glimpse possibilities that weren't available every day.

The fair was not merely about commerce. There was a reason for the time of the fair to be unlike the rest of the year, because it was about devotion to and celebration of the patron saint and of local traditions. On such a holy day, such a holiday, it was appropriate that life should be different from what it was during the rest of the year. The mixture of reverence and license that was associated with the fair might seem a bit contradictory, or even hypocritical.

Still, we are equally likely to mix up reverence with consumption. Americans celebrate George Washington's birthday primarily by shopping at the Presidents' Day clearance sales that have become virtually the only observance of this holiday.

The idea that the fair was a separate time, subject to separate rules, was expanded during the thirteenth century by the Counts of Champagne. At the time, the textile and other emerging industries were making overland commerce particularly important. Old regional fairs were transformed into international events that drew merchants of wool from the west, silk from the south, and furs from the north, along with those selling other goods from all over the continent and beyond.

The towns of Troyes and Provins in the Champagne region of France were logical sites for such important fairs because they were about halfway between Italy and what is now Belgium, which were the centers of the textile industries, and they were also accessible to other trading cities along the North Sea and the Baltic. Nevertheless, they did not dominate by accident. The counts, like many other rulers and religious leaders of the period, recognized that fairs were very powerful moneymaking tools. The owner of the fair could charge a toll to allow people to come to the fair, and also levy a charge for bringing in goods. They could charge for the use of scales and other measures. (The fair at Troyes standardized the troy ounce.) There were also commissions on sales from the buyers and sellers, and the proceeds from fines paid by those who violated the many rules.

Still, none of these revenues would come unless the fairs offered a variety of goods and experiences that couldn't be found anywhere else. Thus the counts declared what became known as "the peace of the fair." They guaranteed protection to anyone on his or her way to the fair, no matter where they were. Their assertion of the peace of the fair was an aggressive act. They promised to retaliate against anyone who prevented a merchant from getting to market, no matter where the attack took place. By making dangerous roads safer, the peace of the fair promoted greater openness and prosperity. It was an assertion that sought to break through the petty warfare and banditry that characterized the continent at the time. It was an attempt to re-create the peace that had once prevailed throughout the Roman world. And it was a precursor to the success of Great Britain in the nineteenth century and of the United States in the twentieth century, in controlling sea lanes, stamping out piracy, and making the world safe for trade.

$\mathcal{M}$arketplace cultures today

Today, most of us spend our lives in a perpetual fair. Someone tries to sell us something nearly every waking moment, and we can buy casually, impersonally, with no wearying negotiation or personal contact. The act of consumption, which was once so exceptional an act in lives dominated by laborious production, is now commonplace and incessant. We are all in the market all the time.

Amid this commercial clamor, some old-style markets endure, and in some places, they are proliferating and prospering. They play only a supporting role in the contemporary buyosphere; few people would care to do all their shopping in markets. But they still offer the possibility of discovery in a place full of sociable strangers.

Markets reflect and define the cultures of the places of which they are a part. A few years ago, I noticed that some of the Pennsylvania and New Jersey farmers who used to sell their fruits and vegetables at Philadelphia's Reading Terminal Market had disappeared. I first assumed that they had sold out their acreage to housing developers, the retirement dream of the East Coast farmer. But shortly after, I saw some of them selling at the Greenmarket in New York's Union Square. The reason was obvious. New Yorkers were willing to pay higher prices, and the farmers found it worthwhile to travel a bit farther to sell their goods.

In the hundred-mile move, though, their goods had changed. In Philadelphia they had sold many of the same items available in a supermarket. In New York, though, there weren't simply tomatoes but heirloom tomatoes in several colors and shapes. The same was true of potatoes. Some farmers in the market specialized in selling the first shoots from vegetables, which are tiny and offer intense concentration of flavor. In Philadelphia, food was primarily sustenance; one hundred miles away in New York, it was fashion, one that was subsequently exported back to Philadelphia. Together, the farmers and the people who shopped in the market transformed the food.

With an economy dominated by software and jet planes, Seattle may be the American city most strongly associated with the contemporary lifestyle. Yet its heart, or perhaps its stomach, is Pike Place Market, a place that is, in its way, as timeless, as sensually exciting and physically memorable as a Persian bazaar. Beginning with stalls overflowing with vegetables piled into carefully engineered pyramids, and fish on ice showing their opalescent skins and fresh, translucent flesh, the market zigzags down a bluff. Used bookstores line the descent toward a vast flea market. The proprietors of these businesses are like those of the Kāshān bazaars, people who spend their lives in the market, and whose survival depends on completing as many transactions as possible. The energy of the market overflows its boundaries, drawing restaurants as neighbors, and inducing people to live nearby.

It's true that in many places, as at London's Covent Garden, real markets have been removed and supplanted by marketlike places that combine historical patina and a promise of authenticity with high prices and modern management. (London still has a few remnants of markets that existed in medieval times, and perhaps before, tucked amid the financial institutions of the City.)

But in other places, markets have sprung up, have been revived, or simply continue to grow. Chinese and other immigrant markets have, for example, brought block after block of outdoor food-selling to Toronto, a city that once seemed destined to be moved entirely indoors. Most big cities have markets, and many have recently become very powerful tourist attractions. But their greater significance may be that they offer both foods and experiences that cannot be found elsewhere.

The supermarkets have been trying, however. Nearly all super-markets welcome shoppers by plunging them directly into their produce departments, to whet their appetites, excite their eyes, and put them in a mood for shopping. Fruits are piled high in wooden baskets even more picturesque than you would find in real markets. Moreover, supermarkets have greatly increased their display of foods that have ethnic connections and an aura of authenticity that is associated with markets. "Gourmet" olive bars seem recently to have materialized in supermarkets everywhere.

Still, it is difficult to reconcile the impersonality and friction-free flow of commodities that make supermarkets work with the tac-tile, emotion-laden world of the market. Supermarket checkers are intentionally uninvolved with the products they sell.

"You call this a lime?" said the checker at my supermarket, hold-ing up a fruit that was, unquestionably, a lime. Later, I pondered how she managed to live into her midtwenties without ever being quite sure of what a lime is, but then, I felt under attack.

"Yes it is," I replied. "They're three for a dollar."

"There ought to be a sticker on it with a number," she retorted. "You should take the ones with the stickers." I shrugged. She began riffling through a booklet, trying to find the code number for a lime, but she didn't seem to really be looking at the pages. She screamed at the checker at the next cash register. "What's this?" she asked.

"Forty–forty-eight," the checker at the next register responded. I realized that to identify it as a lime was completely beside the point. Despite the profusion of greenery and atmospherics, my local supermarket was nothing like a real market.

If I'm going to have a dysfunctional buying experience, I'd prob-ably rather have it in a real market. I often shop at the Italian Mar-ket section of South Philadelphia, where I have an outwardly hostile long-term bad relationship with a vegetable seller. She has sharp features, leathery skin, a scratchy voice, and a short temper. She has looked ancient for the twenty-odd years I have known her, though she never seems to get any older. Sometimes I feel that Aristophanes might have encountered her in the agora. Her prices are very low because her tomatoes are usually very ripe, though sometimes they're rotting. Like the merchants of ancient Greece and since time immemorial, she covers her baskets with beautiful specimens. I wait until her attention is elsewhere and pick up a couple of tomatoes so that I can peer into the basket, but she always catches me.

"I piled those very carefully," she scolds. I knew that, of course. "Take 'em or leave 'em," she snarls. "But don't touch 'em." More often than not I take them, and they are a good buy. She has even begun to give me hints. "You'd better use 'em today" means that I'm probably better off not buying them at all. She has gradually become more helpful, but her anger never seems to abate.

Why do I continue to deal with such an unpleasant woman? It's a mystery, but I suppose I have come to enjoy these prickly encounters. I'd rather fight with her than be scolded because my lime has no ID number.

There's a good reason why we depend on comic writers to tell us about shopping in ancient Greece. The conflicts of the marketplace are petty ones, and they usually end in a deal. Tragic heroes don't get hungry, or haggle over the price. Oedipus never went shopping.

Nevertheless, the market, like the theater, is a special place, separate from the daily routine. Whether you are a buyer or a seller, when you are in the market, you're part of a performance. You're looking. You're learning. You're alive.

4

SELF-EXPRESSION

The Blossoming of the Buyosphere

$\mathcal{T}$he buyosphere is both a set of shopping opportunities and a state of mind. It encompasses the shopping streets of the city, the mall, the supermarket, the home shopping channels, advertisements, and the Internet. But what calls it into being is the willingness and desire of those who inhabit it to imagine their lives differently, to believe that, by making choices, they can express and empower themselves. There are no fixed identities in the buyosphere.

The buyosphere is a place of windows and mirrors. The windows allow us to be voyeurs, glimpsing countless transforming possibilities. Once, the finest things in life were seen only by the powerful. In the buyosphere, everything is on display. You can look at the best, and if you have the money, you can buy it.

The mirrors of the buyosphere help us see ourselves as part of the spectacle, and challenge us to consider what we might become. Few people can go past a mirror without at least glancing at it, and retail designers know that a mirror is always an effective way to slow down the rush of traffic and induce shoppers to look around. Mirrors induce purchasing by forcing us to doubt our own completeness.

In the buyosphere, you spend time considering whether a lamp—or a stuffed boa constrictor—will complete or clutter your living room. Or you try on a garment. "For size," says the sales-clerk. But you know that's a fiction. What you're really trying on is an identity. Most of the time this identity is an enhancement or an extension of one you have already established. But shopping invites us to engage in the play that can lead to self-discovery. "Have I become the sort of man who wears a hat?" you ponder, standing before a mirror, experimenting with ways to reframe your face. It is an idle act, perhaps, an afternoon's diversion. But you buy the hat. Later, when the moment comes to put it on, there are second thoughts. "Is this the hat for me?" you wonder. "Am I the man for this hat?" So the hat remains in the closet, gathering dust. The decisions we make as shoppers aren't always good ones. Still, few people would give up on the possibility of discovering that they are more interesting than they suspect.

Historically, the notion that individuals can create their own identity is fairly new, no more than a few centuries old. It's no accident that this is an idea that took hold at the same time that shopping appeared in a handful of cities. Shopping may not be the highest form of human freedom, but it is the least abstract, most visceral of liberties. By the choices you make—your shoes, your food, your furnishings—you tell the world who you are.

The goods on display in the buyosphere are a mixture of the already popular and the yet-to-be-accepted. What buyers will accept and reject is an enduring mystery, and that's fortunate. It keeps the buyosphere interesting. All who participate in the buyosphere shape its character. What they're wearing and the way they wear it, the way they stand and walk and present themselves to the world are an essential part of its life. The mannequins in the store windows sometimes strike bizarre poses, but they can rarely compete with the body language you find on the street. Personal presentation is far more distinctive and adventurous on a shopping street than in, for example, a courthouse square. Indeed, most of our civic spaces, the ones in which we're supposed to come together as a community, appear monolithic and boring when compared with the buyosphere, a vividly raffish place where you'll find many more kinds of people.

Psychologists have found that our brains are programmed to notice the new. The buyosphere encompasses many long-standing landmarks, but its ceaseless novelty is what makes it a mind-altering drug. That familiar stimulation keeps us coming back again and again.

Because of New York's high-rise character, its buyosphere encompasses a larger percentage of street frontage than it does in other major cities. London, for example, is dominated by houses, and the buyosphere is small in comparison to the endless residential terraces. But in every great city, the buyosphere is where visitors come. They do so not just to purchase things but because such commercial realms are where a city welcomes strangers.

Our contemporary atmosphere of commercial presentation, of buying and selling and posing, is so much a part of contemporary urban life we scarcely notice it. It's as pervasive as the air we breathe. And as with the air, we are more likely to notice its absence. In cities where this activity is absent or suppressed, as it often was, for example, in the former Soviet Bloc countries, the city turns suffocating. A whole layer of life seems to be missing, the brightest and liveliest layer, and what is left are crowds, rush hours, production, and routine.

The buyosphere is the place that invites us to reward ourselves for all the bad things we put up with in life. It is just as important a part of the economy as the assembly line and the accounts-payable department. Nobody makes a profit unless somebody buys, and most major cities are more concerned nowadays with inducing and predicting consumption than they are with manufacturing. The world is awash in abundance. The challenge for sellers is to make each piece of this material plenty mean something, so that shoppers will want to make it part of their lives.

We all know that when the buyosphere welcomes us, it's only after our money. But in order to induce us to spend, it offers flattery, spectacle, and overwhelming variety. And it doesn't sell too hard, because it doesn't want to frighten us away. Retailers have long since learned that the longer we linger, on Fifth Avenue or online, the more money we leave behind.

From marketing to shopping

The evolution of markets into shopping districts, and finally into the inescapable buyosphere in which we live, took a very long time. The changes involved were so subtle and gradual that historians argue whether shopping really began in the sixteenth century, or the eighteenth, or the nineteenth. It all depends, of course, on how restrictively you define shopping, but it seems clear that in at least a handful of sixteenth-century European cities you can see the beginnings of the buyosphere. This first blossoming came not as a result of retail trading practices, but rather from a change in the way people imagined themselves and the societies of which they were part.

Today, the medieval concept of the hierarchy of creation, with God at the top and rocks at the bottom, with angels, clergy, nobles, peasants and animals in between, would strike most people as too primitive an idea to inspire deep conviction. Yet this idea of an ordered creation underlay a system in which survival depended not on making money but on doing one's duty. The nobility was seen to have an obligation to the peasants, just as parents do to their children, and likewise, the peasants had a duty to the nobles. It may have occurred to some peasants that they were doing a great deal for their landlords and not getting very much in return, but that would have been a stray thought, not a worldview. This obligation-based conception of society viewed worldly survival not as an individual matter, but as a collective one. A good relationship between all the parts of the society was seen to bring harmony and prosperity, a bad one famine and bloodshed.

One can't help feeling, though, that in European cities of the late sixteenth and seventeenth centuries, and especially in London, people started to become a lot more like us. They saw themselves not as part of a stable cosmic order, but rather as actors in a lively, very worldly drama in which the outcome was in doubt. They began to see themselves as works in progress, capable of changing to take advantage of new opportunities. They began to think a lot about making choices. The people who were thinking this way were, at first, a very small group, but the transformation they began remade cities and redefined people's ambitions.

The change was not just about trade. Even large and frequent fairs like the ones held in Troyes and Provins in the Champagne region of France did not make these cities lastingly important or begin the development of shopping districts. What made the buyosphere happen was power. Shopping arose in cities to which people felt that they needed to come and in which they felt it was essential to be impressive.

The great fairs represented an important transitional stage. The next step was the establishment by a number of kings, dukes, financiers, and institutions, of lavishly intimidating seats of power. You went to the king in his court, or to the Medicis in Florence, or to the Vatican in Rome because you wanted something: a grant of privilege, for example, or a loan. Eventually, you went merely to protect your interest, to make sure that those who were in the court would not gain any privileges at your expense.

Those drawn to these seats of power were, for the most part, wealthy people who controlled vast tracts of land. They had something to gain or something to lose. Traditionally, these were the people who had long been at the center of power and culture of the territory over which they held sway. Compared with the peasants around them, they were magnificent. But as the courts and leading households in the most powerful cities became increasingly refined and ostentatious, these rural gentry began to transform themselves, by choice or necessity, into courtiers.

In the powerful cities, there was a proliferation of luxury craftsmen, often people who practiced old crafts for new purposes. For example, even though sixteenth-century noblemen were far less likely to go off to battle in a suit of armor than their grandfathers had been, there was an explosion of armor-making. This new armor was not so much intended for protection of the body as for the projection of an image. Like a Porsche or a Ferrari nowadays, it was an ostensibly practical object that was largely an assertion of potency and an affirmation of wealth.

Clothing is, of course, a more flexible and subtly expressive form of armor. For the rural noble on his manor to know what was being worn in court that year, he had little choice but to go to London, Paris, or Florence to see what people were wearing and get his own clothes made or at least brought up to date. Thus in every place where there was a powerful court, there arose a coterie of cloth-sellers, tailors, hatters, boot-makers, hosiery-knitters, feather merchants, sword-makers, jewelers, perfumers, and many others to serve what proved to be a growing clientele. (Painters and sculptors, too, were among the skilled artisans who were given new opportunities by this Renaissance elaboration of court life.)

The places where these people did business were not stores but rather workshops, or, in the case of the cloth merchants, small warehouses. Everything was made to measure and to order. Most of the people who worked in the shops spent most of their time producing the objects, and only a small part of their time consulting with customers. The idea of browsing didn't yet exist; what you saw in a shop were tools, apprentices, and partially completed goods others had ordered. Anyone who walked in was virtually committed to be a buyer, though the shop-owner would help you figure out exactly what you wanted and could afford. By twenty-first-century standards, clothing was extremely expensive, a major investment. You wanted to make sure that you had made the right decision.

More than one thousand years before, in ancient Rome, there had also been a class of wealthy people who sought to impress their peers and win political favor. But in those times, those who made and sold luxury items almost always came to their customers' houses to do business and deliver their goods. In Renaissance Europe, by contrast, the buyers nearly always visited the artisans' shops. This transformed such purchasing into a semipublic activity. It brought luxury and display out of the courts and onto the streets. As in marketplaces, those selling similar goods and services tended to cluster in the same district. And a handful of artisans, including those who sold gold and decorative items, began to make small displays of their wares.

Shopping began with the nobles and gentry, who were feeling insecure about their roles, and realized they had to perform in the increasingly theatrical royal and ducal courts where power was exercised. But it soon spilled out of the courts and began to be visible on the street. Eventually this would give rise to a new kind of insecurity, as people of low social position became wealthy and were able to afford the same goods, or better ones, than the nobles purchased.

Over time, these districts of high-quality artisans became known as attractions of the cities in which they were located. Particular specialties became associated with certain cities. Milan became so famous for its ribbons and other decorative clothing items that retailers selling such items in other cities became known as millinery shops. And after some prominent Venetian glassblowers moved to Paris, for example, that city became known as a center for perfume, a product whose container is always as important as its contents.

In London, during the reign of Queen Elizabeth I at the end of the sixteenth century, courtiers who, like their counterparts elsewhere rarely bathed, became enamored of Parisian scents. They purchased their fragrances from merchants who obtained them from Paris, or who at least claimed that they did. In London, as in many other places where this sort of ostentation was taking hold, the most prestigious items were ones that had been imported, that were, their sellers boasted, "far-fetched." On the outskirts of the city, there were many cloth-weavers and others who made a good living crafting high-quality goods that commanded higher prices when sold as imports.

Queen Elizabeth I herself is remembered both as the chief ornament of this court and as a skillful and ruthless manipulator of court intrigue. But she apparently had mixed feelings about the attraction of her court. Members of the nobility, she felt, should spend less time preening and scheming in London and more time at home. Those who were spending their wealth on plumed hats and silk doublets had a traditional obligation to dispense charity to those who worked and lived on their estates. They apparently felt less of a duty to be charitable to those they rarely saw. The queen worried about the disappearance of what might nowadays be termed a social safety net in the countryside. But she was unable to dim the pull of London.

In some ways, the greater visibility and public importance of shopping in London, compared with other cities of the time, was established even before Elizabeth's reign when Sir Thomas Gresham opened the Royal Exchange in 1567. His intent was not so much to encourage retail trade as to provide a selling and trading place for foreign merchants. At that time, most such business was done on the street, or when the weather was bad, inside St. Paul's Cathedral. The Royal Exchange was a two-story building, built around a courtyard, with spaces on the ground floor set aside for traders from abroad. The upper arcade contained shops. While the exchange did not become quite the international center Gresham had envisioned, it became a central place for the exchange of news and gossip. Thus, while the shops had initially been very difficult to rent, the traffic soon made them highly desirable. This forerunner to the shopping mall remained one of London's top locations for well over a century.

Unlike in France, where the new luxury trades were directly under the control of the king and nobility, in London, this new commercial activity affected a large segment of the population. One important factor was that the city itself had grown dramatically in size. In 1640, on the eve of the civil war, London's population was estimated at three hundred thousand, more than five times what it had been a century before. This influx overwhelmed the old guild regulations that governed how artisans were trained, what they could make, and what they could sell. Many of these people skipped apprenticeship and worked for wages, or opened businesses of their own.

To meet the demand, they began to sell items made by others as well. There had long been merchants called haberdashers, whose small shops were typically filled floor to ceiling with bells, dishes, paper, bowstrings, thread, buttons, and countless other kinds of small items, none of which were produced on the premises. There were also grocers, whose inventory included spices and other edible items, but no fresh food. As these various businesses became larger, they offered items that overlapped with those of other sorts of merchants and, more significantly, with the artisan-retailers. Before long, even some of the artisans began selling things they hadn't made themselves. These varied shops were so useful and convenient that the concept of retail trade began to lose most of its stigma, and the status of "shopman" became almost respectable.

One of the things that these new, miscellaneous shops of the Elizabethan era sold was patent medicine, preparations packed in distinctly shaped bottles, and usually wrapped in printed testimonials to their effectiveness in treating a wide array of complaints. Alcohol was usually their chief ingredient. Except for some surgery, most medical practice of the time was less than useless, and the most common response to illness was prayer. In fact, most patent medicines that weren't actively dangerous worked on the same principle as prayer: Belief in their effectiveness was their most active ingredient. Yet the use of a patent medicine reflects a very different state of mind from prayer. It means that you are taking some responsibility for your own survival. You live not just at God's pleasure, but as a result of your own determination.

The pull of fashionable London became even stronger during the reign of Elizabeth's successor, James I, who seems to have believed in the royal pretension to grandeur in a way that, one suspects, the shrewder queen never did. The theatricality of the court became more blatant, as one can see in Rubens's depiction of the king as Apollo on the ornate ceiling of the Banqueting House in Whitehall. The capital was drawing not just the nobility, but others of more moderate means who were on the make. Ben Jonson, who composed court masques in addition to his cynical comedies, knew these people well. As one of his characters observes: "To be an accomplished gentleman—that is a gentleman of the time—you must give over housekeeping in the country and live altogether in the City among gallants, where, at your first appearance t'were good you turned four or five acres of your land into two or three trunks of apparel." Since land was, at the time, the basis of all wealth, this was a serious sacrifice for a couple of suits of clothes. Thus, although Jonson's observation carries with it more than a hint of disapproval, he was aware that times were changing. One could not rely simply on being a gentleman; you had to be a gentleman of the time.

This was the time when Shakespeare's plays were written, and his characters may have been the first to reflect the reality that people no longer were assigned to a fixed role in the society. By acquiring the manners, the learning, and, above all, the wardrobe, they could become new sorts of people. Shakespeare's characters do not seem to be victims of fate, or heroes on quests whose outcome, while in doubt, is also predetermined. Prince Hal makes a conscious decision to change his character, while Hamlet seems to be making up his tragedy as he goes along. And in Shakespeare, disguises always work; every character who poses as someone else gets away with it easily. If you change your costume, you can change your role in life. That's what happens on the stage, and in Shakespeare's London it was happening in the court and on the streets as well.

Early New York: An outpost of the buyosphere

In the seventeenth century, New York was a tiny, rather insignificant place, a symptom of Europeans' growing acquisitiveness. The town existed because Europeans wanted things, and they were willing to go to the ends of the earth to get them. The earliest history of New York, when it was Nieuw Amsterdam, a small Dutch settlement whose northern boundary was Wall Street, seems to offer a prelude to the well-developed buyosphere of today. An out-post that had been created to tap a continent's treasures, New York was, in its small way, rich from the beginning. And its markets, institutions designed to deal with scarcity, were instead over-whelmed by abundance.

Like nearly all the settlements in North America, New York was a commercial venture, though unlike Puritan New England and Quaker Pennsylvania, it had no other aim than to make money. It was a company town, set up by the Dutch West India Company to purchase furs and other goods cheaply from the Indians and a handful of frontier hunters and trappers, then sell them expensively in Europe. The settlers were expected to buy most of what they needed from a company store, where prices were kept high both to maintain profits and to discourage the settlers from becoming too self-indulgent. At that time, even people who were sellers of luxury goods saw buying things to be, if not exactly sinful, a sign of weak character. And merchants tend to be skeptical of free trade when-ever they don't think they will be able to control it.

This system worked during the first few years after the colony was established as a trading post in 1626, but a decade later, after the company induced Dutch farmers and artisans to settle there, the regime of the company store began to break down. The Dutch problem wasn't the scarcity of food that had bedeviled the Pilgrims in Plymouth in 1620, but rather the abundance of goods that was available to the settlers. The early Dutch descriptions of the colony's plenitude read like verbal still-lifes, with lengthy descrip-tions of the snails, the mussels, the oysters, the game. There are accounts of lobsters five-feet long (though those one- to two-feet long are deemed best for eating) and of dozens of different kinds of edible fowl and game. Some of this is very likely exaggerated, an early bit of real-estate promotion. But New York *was* very different in those days, as one early court case shows. It involved a man who had chased a bear from the banks of the East River clear across town to the Hudson, where a boy shot it. The question was who should get the skin, the chaser or the shooter.

The site of the Dutch colony at the tip of Manhattan Island was uniquely accessible by water from several different directions, so Indians from several tribes, as well as English settlers from Connecticut and Dutch from outside of the settlement could converge there, selling or trading game, fresh fish, livestock, and various kinds of goods to the settlers.

The company's response was to set up an official market, so that those who wanted to trade would come at particular times and the buying and selling would be subject to scrutiny and taxation. This worked for a while, but, ultimately, the sheer abundance of goods overwhelmed the market. Those with goods to trade came on non-market days. The Dutch, like the English, began using the shell money used by the Indians, because it was a convenient, low-value currency, and many of the best goods could be purchased with it. The Dutch then set up another market at a spot where the Indians sold their freshly caught fish, and then another market and yet another to serve people who found the official markets inconveniently distant and were trading instead with people who had come to them.

In England and many other European countries at the time, markets were forbidden to open near other existing markets. But the Dutch and later the English kept opening markets in Manhattan within a short distance of one another, seemingly to uphold the illusion that commerce was properly under control. But really, it wasn't. The entire settlement was turning into a market, without boundaries, hours, or someone in charge. And people from all over have been coming to Manhattan to sell things ever since.

An explosion of belongings

The material elaboration of life during the century between 1625 and 1725 was a striking international phenomenon. We can look, for example, at paintings of Dutch domestic interiors over that time span. With each year that goes by, the rooms in the paintings seem to fill up with more and more stuff. Bare floors give way to straw mats that are superseded by Persian and Turkish carpets, which have moved from tables to the floor. Chairs become softer, cabinets larger. Moreover, the objects in earlier pictures are often placed there purely for their symbolism; the more elaborate furnishings of later works, though they might still be symbolic, also function as marks of prestige and contributors to homely comfort. Although they contain allegories about the vanity of human endeavor, the paintings tell us that the subjects were doing very well, thank you. Admittedly, those whose rooms were painted were wealthier than average, but as estate inventories and other documents tell us, increasing numbers of people were living more lavish lives.

Many of the items of domestic life that we now take for granted first appeared during this period. One of them was the innovation that the French called a *commode,* because it was convenient, but which the English called a chest of drawers. The name tells us that it replaced simple chests, which were opened from the top. The existence of such a large and expensive piece of furniture tells us that people were purchasing a large enough number of clothes and linens—and that they were sufficiently fussy about the way they were stored and handled—to make so large an expenditure prudent.

Another item that was rare in the seventeenth century but commonplace by the eighteenth was the fork. Its appearance was part of a whole shift of manners that required a large amount of new paraphernalia for eating that had not been required before. Food had been served on tin or pewter platters, and the diners used their hands, spoons, and whatever knives they happened to be carrying. The idea of the individual place setting, in which each diner had a plate, a fork, and a knife to call his own was a novelty, even among the well-to-do.

Some observers have argued that the transformation of the meal from a collective, yet somewhat competitive, endeavor to an individual entitlement coincided with a general awareness that famine had ceased to be an immediate threat. It seems, at least, to have been part of a more general trend toward awareness of oneself as a distinct individual. That same impulse underlay the increasing attention given to personal style in dress. The more you feel that you are on your own and must make your own way, the more things you are likely to buy to lend yourself authority.

The introduction of coffee, tea, and chocolate into Western Europe triggered a further shopping boom, in the form of cups, spoons, pots, linens, and other accoutrements of a new social ritual. These drinks were imported products, primarily from China, as were many of the items used to serve them. Because they were served hot, drinking them from the pewter or leather tankards most people owned would burn the fingers. But the proliferation of tea and coffee paraphernalia went far beyond the merely utilitarian. Before large numbers of ceramic plates and cups began to be imported from Asia, there had been little production of pottery for eating in Europe. The pottery industries of England and Holland, especially, grew up in order to emulate and compete with the imports. And the greater delicacy that serving tea encouraged was also a boon to silversmiths, who began to produce large quantities of spoons and later pots and other serving pieces.

Clocks, though rarer, proliferated during this period. Time, previously defined by a single clock at the center of a town or village, became a personal, or at least a household possession. We can also assume that it was becoming increasingly important, though the coming of the industrial system that made them essential was still in the future. (In contemporary households, of course, the trend has gone completely haywire; there are clocks everywhere. What was once a great luxury has become a minor nuisance.)

English estate inventories of the period provide important evidence of how people were changing. In 1675, the looking glass, that fundamental instrument of egotism, was a household rarity. This isn't surprising. Mirrors were made from glass and silver, both relatively expensive materials. Nevertheless, by the mid-1720s, mirrors were commonplace in all households with any pretension. To look upon oneself in a mirror is to worry about how you appear to others. To consider changing or improving that appearance is a small mental leap, one that implicitly relates to purchases you might make.

"I find I must go handsomely, whatever it costs me, and the charge will be made up in the fruit it brings." So wrote Samuel Pepys in his diary, remarking on the large part of his time and fortune that was devoted to choosing, updating, and repairing his wardrobe. Pepys was a man about town, to be sure, and he is remembered for the detail and candor with which he recorded the events of his life. He was not, however, noble, or even a very important person. In the late seventeenth century, worrying about fashion and being preoccupied with your appearance was still something that concerned men far more than women. And many more men worried about it than ever before. That doesn't mean the majority of them did; most were poor and had few hopes of ever becoming anything else. A growing number, though, saw themselves as people with opportunities. They couldn't be secure about their future, although there were some grounds for optimism. So, like most people today, they believed that it was worthwhile to dress and live in a way intended to excite admiration and command respect. Like Pepys, they went shopping and spent more than they should have.

Prices of clothing remained extremely high during this period, and consumed a far higher percentage of the income of a man like Pepys than would be true for even the most ardent devotee of fashion today. There was also an active market for used clothing, and the high value made it very attractive to steal. Thieves often used long fishpole-like devices with hooks at the end, which they put through open windows to see what they could catch. There were two districts of the city filled with secondhand clothing merchants, a boon to thieves and to newcomers who arrived in London with more ambition than money (with the notable exception of the plague epidemic, when the clothes flooding the shops proved to be deadly).

Travelers in seventeenth-century London were enormously impressed by the shops. "There is no City in the World that has so many and such fine shops," wrote a French visitor in 1663, a few years after the restoration of the monarchy. "For they are larger and their decorations are as valuable as those on the stage." Other visitors were greatly impressed with the aggregation of goldsmiths to be found on a street called Cheapside. Actually, it was the goldsmiths' wives who exerted most of the fascination. They stood on the doorsteps, urging passersby into the shops. People were accustomed to screaming fishwives, hawking salted fish from door to door. But the well-dressed, seemingly respectable goldsmiths' wives out on the street soliciting business was a novelty, and based on men's reactions, a fairly titillating one.

Display was rudimentary by contemporary standards. Sellers of cloth, for example, would drape fabric to give potential customers a sense of how it might look in a coat, a dress, or a wall hanging. Often such displays were placed so that they could be seen through the small-paned windows of the shop, but for the most part, inventory was displayed in a great jumble in the shop window and all through the store.

English estate inventories of the early 1700s suggest that, while those who had enough possessions to be worth listing still constituted a minority of the total population, both the number of such people and the number of items they possessed steadily rose throughout the period. Moreover, London no longer completely dominated the country's consumption. By 1725, many of the new amenities of life were just as common in provincial cities as they were in the capital. Merchants liked to display the coats of arms of their royal and noble customers, but it was not the court so much as a growing domestic market that had a much-changed sense of itself that was sustaining this great material expansion.

While what was found in London, and increasingly in other important European cities, was far from modern retailing, nearly everyone recognized that something new and important was happening. Clusters of stores were coming together to form linear miles of shopping. Buying fine goods had once been an elite and private act. Now it was a semipublic activity, to which an increasing percentage of the population could aspire. The buyosphere developed quickly and nearly overwhelmed the city. By 1725, a survey found that fully one quarter of the houses in London were occupied by either shops or taverns.

Restricting shopping to preserve order

Other places in Europe, the Americas, and Asia felt the impact of the same commercial dynamism, new money, and changing sense of self and status that transformed the streets and parlors of seventeenth-century England and Holland. Many rulers understood these changes to be a threat to the established social hierarchy—and ultimately to their own legitimacy. If the most desirable objects were to fall into the wrong hands, that would show that high rank counted for nothing, and everything could be bought. Thus, the rulers attempted to control and limit the manufacture and distribution of both traditionally prestigious and newly fashionable items. They hoped that public display and consumption would play its traditional role of bolstering the regime, rather than undermining it.

The difficulties of making such a strategy work were most apparent in France, one of the world's most powerful nations, and one that had a long history of making articles that were desired throughout the world. During the 1600s, Paris had all the prerequisites to be a great center of shopping: advanced industries, innovative craftspeople, an interest in fashion, an influx of money.

But the ambitions of Paris were thwarted by the fears of Versailles, where the royal court defined the extremes of luxury and the heights of taste. The kings and their ministers took this responsibility seriously. In addition to running royal factories that made fine objects for use in the court and by nobles, the central government promulgated rules on manufacture. These defined which guilds of craftsmen would make each category of object, as well as where and to whom they would be sold. These laws were justified as the only way to properly allocate the nation's wealth and preserve the social order. They became an insanely complex body of regulations that sparked incessant contention and infighting. Many items could be sold in one town, or one neighborhood, but not another. Guilds competed with one another to get the privilege of making the most fashionable and profitable objects, and their leaders intrigued with and bribed bureaucrats to allow them to do so.

Those enforcing the laws had a particularly difficult time dealing with innovation in manufacture, technology, and retailing. People were creating new things to buy. The umbrella, for example, was a new product that became stylish and useful. Government officials wrestled with issues of whether they should allow a new industry of umbrella-makers, or perhaps give the franchise to one of the other guilds whose products were less in demand and needed new product lines to employ all their members. (Regulating innovation is always difficult, as has been proven once again in the Microsoft antitrust case. The central issue there—was the Web browser a new product or an improvement of an existing one?—is similar to those that bedeviled French officials.)

New, more efficient ways of making things also created opportunities for bourgeois Parisians, but headaches for the administrators. Hosiery, for example, had long been extremely expensive and limited to the nobility. Methods that brought the price down made it more popular, but the system wasn't designed to cope with such change. The places where such products could be sold and the prices that could be charged continued to be restricted. Such regulations pushed much commerce out of buildings and onto the streets. Many more people were able to afford fine things, and they found ways of obtaining them. Like that of their counterparts in other large European cities, their money was going farther. Estate records indicate that while the value of what people bequeathed remained constant, the number of items in their legacies greatly increased.

Throughout the 1600s and 1700s, administrators struggled to contain both innovation and demand. Meanwhile, Paris began to develop a buyosphere despite them. But unlike in Amsterdam or London, in Paris shopping for nice things was both an act of self-indulgence and a political gesture, a low-key form of rebellion.

A world away, in Japan, court administrators were having much the same problem. Trade with the rest of the world was enriching artisans, who were able to command large sums by exporting their wares, and creating a new class of merchants. Expansion of sea trade even helped peasants, who were getting higher prices for their crops. For the shoguns who ruled the country, this increasing wealth was threatening. Unlike in Europe, where the nobility had income from the land, the samurai nobles depended for their money on the shogun. It seemed that they were the only people in the country who were living on a fixed income. The shoguns' response was to enact sumptuary laws, closely regulating what members of each class were permitted to wear and own.

"Fashions have changed from those of the past and have become increasingly ostentatious," wrote Ihara Saikaku of his compatriots in late-seventeenth-century Japan. "In everything people have a liking for finery above their station. . . . Because they forget their proper place, extravagant women should be in fear of divine punishment."

The result was a flurry of regulation. Restrictions were placed on wedding presents, on what could be served at banquets, on the number of horses one could own. Just about every aspect of life was subject to numerical limits, and when these didn't work, the shogun simply issued some more. In the year 1683 alone, seven sumptuary laws were passed. One specified all the items of clothing town-dwelling merchants or artisans were allowed to have. Another forbade the use of embroidery in women's clothes, though this was rescinded soon after because, as the legislation rescinding the ruling noted, nobody was following the regulation. A second law of 1683 required jail terms for those wearing gorgeous clothes inappropriate for their station, while yet another imposed penalties on merchants who sold fine silks at high prices to merchants and artisans, rather than at lower prices for the nobility.

It seems, when you read about it now, a hopeless, even comical situation. Yet Japan's rulers persisted until the nineteenth century in imposing sumptuary laws in a largely vain attempt to ensure that luxurious clothes and furnishings were acquired only by those who had a right to them. In one sense, though, these rulers succeeded; they remained in charge.

The consequences of choice

We live now in a world of countless choices, most of them unexciting. We complain that the politicians who are running for office offer only an uninspiring choice. Or that the breakfast cereals at the supermarket are all overpriced and boring. We forget that for most of human history, most people didn't feel that they had any choices.

In seventeenth-century England, people began to feel that they had many choices. They could choose scents, and bear grease to slick down their hair. They could go into a shop and choose fine brocades. They could choose their religion and dress all in black. They executed one king, then deposed and replaced another.

The English seventeenth century, that great age of shopping and of science, was also the most politically tumultuous of that country's history. This may seem a weird mixture of trivial and consequential choices; most would probably view political or religious choices to be weightier than buying draperies or hair-grooming preparations. Nevertheless, a breaking down of sumptuary restrictions—thus challenging the idea that social roles are fixed—is almost always the first step in the expansion of freedom.

Shopping doesn't substitute for other sorts of choice, nor should it provide the model for all other kinds of choice. We shouldn't choose a leader the way we choose a shampoo. (Though voters do seem to pay a lot of attention to hairstyle and what the candidate wears. Proper self-presentation is still a path to power.) And the citizens of some of the former Soviet Bloc countries have discovered that a simple lust for goods leads to racketeering and corruption, and the loss of meaningful choice. Shopping is decidedly not the same as democracy.

Yet the first choice people are able to make is always, in some sense, a consumer choice. The chief of the tribe or the king of the country is defined by what he wears and by the valuables he possesses. When we stop being primarily members of the tribe or subjects of the king, we have to define ourselves, and we do it in much the same way, by the clothes we wear and the things we have.

Choice begins on the commercial streets, out in the buyosphere. All of us have but one life to live, and we know that much of our ability to realize our ambitions depends on how we look, what we have, what we buy.

5

INSECURITY

Fashion and the Quest for a Great Buy

*E*arly one rainy morning several years ago, the phone rang, and I was awakened to a great buying opportunity. The Buten Museum of Wedgwood was being liquidated, a friend told me. Everything would be sold. But if we didn't get out there immediately, the opportunity would be lost.

I didn't need to give the offer a moment's thought. Quickly, I got dressed, picked up my friend and was off to the sale. It was, after all, a once-in-a-lifetime opportunity. How often does a museum have a going-out-of-business sale? Museums often excite the impulse to acquire, and nearly all have shops. But you never get a chance to buy the collection itself.

Still, there was no good reason for me to be so eager to get to the sale. For one thing, I had never in my fifteen years in Philadelphia visited this museum, or even intended to do so. Wedgwood china had never been something that much interested me. Moreover, I had no shortage of dishes, while I did have a shortage of places for storing my dishes. Nevertheless, I braved the torrential rain and a small legion of similarly greedy people to have the chance to buy items that I didn't need and that had never interested me before. And, I need hardly add, I bought some Wedgwood.

Most people are able to convince themselves, at least temporarily, that it is absolutely crucial to buy items they don't really need. Indeed, our economic health depends on shoppers' ceaseless lust for the inessential. By historical standards, even relatively poor people in most developed countries live overabundant lives. They have closets full of clothes, cabinets full of dishes, cupboards containing expensively processed foods, and living rooms with furniture and decorative items. And members of the middle class generally have everything they need—even if they don't really believe it.

Some critics of our rich, perhaps wasteful, lifestyle argue that we are simply being tricked by marketers and advertisers to buy into our own destruction. There's no doubt that individuals are being bombarded with more commercial come-ons than ever before, and while any sane person has to ignore most of them, a few each day probably have an effect.

Still, it is difficult to believe that people shop and buy things simply because they have been duped. Shoppers are not zombies. They think about what they do. They strategize. They compare. They work at it. If there is a cabal to induce people to consume wastefully, shoppers are, at the very least, coconspirators.

Advertising helps create insecurity by convincing its targets that there is something missing in their lives that only the product being offered can satisfy. But, to a considerable degree, we choose the insecurities to which we care to respond. And we create insecurities of our own that induce us to buy things because we crave change, progress, excitement, and a feeling of accomplishment.

In one sense, you could say that my rush to buy Wedgwood proved that marketing works. Wedgwood has been a prestige name in pottery for more than two and a half centuries. I had never been particularly interested in the company's wares, but I certainly had heard of them, and so has everyone else. My everyday dishes—Pottery Barn circa 1978—were beginning to look both dated and immature. I realized that I was feeling insecure both because my plates were out of fashion and because they might communicate that I was not making the sort of progress I should be making in life. Buying Wedgwood could assuage this insecurity both because it purports to be timeless and because the pottery is inarguably a grown-up possession. Middle age is a serious time that calls for serious dishes.

Thus, fashion was one of the forces that impelled my purchases. The other was an even more powerful drive that came from an even deeper insecurity: the fear of missing out on something special. Scarcity is the spice of shopping. And even though we may be awash in goods, we are still capable of convincing ourselves that if we don't buy now, a unique opportunity will be lost.

For a short time—long enough to make the purchase—I was able to convince myself that purchasing Wedgwood could be a life-transforming experience, and that if I missed out, something irredeemable would be lost. Both of these may have been illusions. If I hadn't bought the dishes, my life would not have been different. But I do not for a moment regret the purchases. The quest for them was fun, the plates are attractive, and the price was low. They were, in other words, what every shopper is looking for: a great buy.

ᵐManufacturing insecurity

Wedgwood is a product of mid–eighteenth-century England. For many who appreciate well-designed, well-crafted objects, the eighteenth century holds a special place. It was the first time that fine goods were widely available, so refinement and gentility could become an aspiration for much of the population. And it was the last time that things were typically made by hand by skilled artisans, before factories and machine production would make things more abundant but much less fine. It was the last gasp of an ancien régime of unquestioned good taste and sturdy cabinetry.

This view is a crude oversimplification. The vast and growing enthusiasm for cloth, especially brightly printed cotton, was already driving the mechanization of the textile industry and the beginnings of the industrial revolution. It changed how people saw their lives and how they made their livings. A mixed blessing, industrialization made cities vastly larger, air and water dirtier, and goods far more abundant. Europe's lust for inexpensive cotton garments perpetuated American slavery, a legacy that haunts us still. Nevertheless, few would wish to return to a pre-industrial world of shorter lives and real scarcities. The industrial revolution represents the dividing line between a world in which goods were scarce and important, and one in which they were abundant and often trivial. It brought a world full of stuff in which uncertainty itself had to be manufactured.

It's difficult to write about this period without getting caught up in a long-running chicken-and-egg argument. For a long time, most historians believed that the invention of new methods of production preceded large-scale consumption. They usually ignored the elaboration of house interiors and personal wardrobes among a visible minority of the population and the increasing commercialization of the street.

Later historians reversed this vision, arguing that nothing less than a consumer revolution preceded and caused the industrial revolution that followed. Some recent scholars, in turn, have criticized this analysis, saying that those who went shopping before the industrial revolution were a tiny elite compared with the masses who were able to do so afterward. People became consumers, this argument goes, only as a consequence of industrialization, as manufacturers found ways to induce and predict demand, and as the people learned to accept industrial products in place of any larger sense of meaning in their lives.

This may seem an arcane scholarly debate, but it has implications for the way we shop, and indeed, for the way we understand our lives. Is our shopping an exercise in freedom and self-definition, a consequence of the expansion of powers and insecurities of the individual that began during the Renaissance? Or is shopping a kind of compulsive behavior that helps compensate for the fact that our lives are meaningless and unsatisfying? Do we fill up our homes with stuff because we are empty within?

In this book, and especially in the previous chapter, I have been making the first of these arguments. It seems obvious that people have used material goods throughout history and before not as substitutes for meaning but as expressions of power, affirmations of relationships, and extensions of themselves. Moreover, it stands to reason that as people increasingly came to see the society, and eventually the universe, as fluid rather than fixed, increasing numbers of people would seek to assert themselves through goods. In France, the crown tried to preserve a monopoly over luxury and taste. In Japan, the rulers fought mightily to prevent status goods from being used by those of lower station. In England, there were some efforts to prevent inappropriate acquisition and display, but, for several reasons, it was allowed, and England proved to be the leader in moving on to the next step: industrialization that made shoppers of a far larger percentage of the population.

There is little doubt that the investments in organization and machinery required for an industrial revolution would not have been made if there were no demand for its products. At the same time, though, it would be naïve to deny that the industrial revolution re-created and transformed the consumer. The enormously increased ability to produce goods made the shopper part of the machine. Industrialization enabled a far larger portion of the society to buy things. But industrialization intrinsically requires people to keep on buying things again and again in predictable ways. It cannot afford to allow people to be satisfied, for that threatens prosperity. A penny spent must be spent again and again for everyone to become richer in the process. Avarice and happiness never meet, Benjamin Franklin said, but an industrial society inevitably encourages its members to want more and more. Like a bicycle, it can only stand up when it is in motion. Fashion is one of the things that makes the machinery go.

The uses of fashion

Fashion is one way to render goods obsolete before their useful lives are over. Thus fashion plays an important role in adding feelings of scarcity and insecurity to a world of factory-made abundance. It can make a warm and useful coat unwearable, a sturdy and comfortable chair dowdy. It feels like a way of engaging the future, but its chief impact is to make people dissatisfied with the present, and especially with all the objects in it.

Still, fashion is a far older phenomenon than industrialization. "The fashion wears out more apparel than the man." So wrote Shakespeare, in *Much Ado About Nothing,* about a century and a half before the onset of industrialization. And fashion was a force long before Shakespeare's time. We are aware of waves of fashion sweeping through at least the upper reaches of societies far into ancient times. There have been fashions in hairstyles, in clothing, in names, in dogs, fashions in the way people stand, sit, and recline; fashions in what parts of the body to reveal and what parts to cover. They have not always moved as fast nor affected so many people as they do now. But fashions are like the seasons. They are about change, recurrence, and life going on.

Fashion isn't a conspiracy against shoppers by manufacturers to get them to buy more things. Or, at least, that's not all it is. It is also a measure and expression of the eventfulness of life. We may be embarrassed by the shoulder pads, shag carpets, harvest-green refrigerators, permed hair, tailfins, poodle skirts, or saddle shoes of bygone eras. But to have experienced all these things, to have made them part of our lives, is one of the ways in which we can feel ourselves to be part of history. The timeless lives of peasants, who have lived for centuries using the same objects and performing the same tasks as their ancestors and descendents, were profoundly boring. Experiencing change can be challenging, but we mustn't forget that it is also a privilege.

Fashion is artificial. It is created by clothing designers in Paris and Milan, and by committees of building-materials manufacturers who gather regularly in New York to coordinate their colors, hoping that everyone will yearn for new kitchen counters. Yet it is also deeply mysterious. It is difficult to see where it is going, and even harder to understand who forms taste and how they do it. A magazine like *Vogue* suggests that it comes from designers, while *In Style* seems to demonstrate that it is shaped by celebrities. Most sociologists and historians who have written on the subject have tended to assume that fashion is driven by elite groups, and especially by the aspirations of prosperous people to be accepted as members of the taste-making class.

It would be foolish to deny that class plays a big role when we go shopping. Which objects are expensive and which brands are prestigious are data that most people seem to learn without even trying. But that doesn't mean that we go shopping in the hope of being someone we're not. More often, we acquire a thing in the hopes of expressing, or even discovering, who we really are. Fashion is the way in which we participate in culture, even in a culture that tells us that the highest value is to be an individual.

In recent years, companies that sell shoes and clothing to a worldwide youth market have sent scouts to some of the poorest neighborhoods around the world, photographing how people wear their clothes and documenting the handwriting on the wall. The underclass and the mainstream have been trading looks for a long time, but never more clearly than in the last two decades.

Even those who don't consider themselves creatures of fashion can't help but notice and be influenced, if only in subtle and nearly indiscernible ways. Even items that claim to transcend fashion are shaped by it. When the models on the runways are wearing dresses that brush the floor, even the most "classic" styles will go a little longer. And when the latest neckties become big as bibs or thin as strings, the most conservative ones will grow or shrink by an eighth of an inch. Thus even clothes intended to appear inconspicuous must follow fashions; if they are way out of style, they stand out and fail in their purpose.

Wedgwood appeals today because of its aura of timelessness, which is, in fact, illusory. The company would not have lasted as long as it did if it failed to respond to changing tastes in color and design. (One of the plates I bought had swoopy 1950s designs on it. It was something I had never imagined: populuxe Wedgwood.)

And in its early years, the business was a pioneer in manipulating and creating fashions to sell more goods.

Designing a product and a culture

Josiah Wedgwood, who founded his pottery firm in 1759, was one of the first to marry stylish goods with factory production. Unlike the French porcelain-makers at Sèvres, who operated under the direct patronage of the king and whose products embodied the taste of the court, Wedgwood was on his own, and he had to serve a broader market. Perhaps his most important competitors were the porcelain makers of China. They had been mass-producing high-quality ceramics for centuries, and they were willing to provide just about anything a European customer cared to order, whether in Chinese or European taste. Wedgwood surmounted this challenge by creating a style that was recognizably his own, and then creating a taste for it.

Wedgwood's first great success was to sell a very large set of his dishes to Queen Charlotte in 1765. The idea that one could own exactly the same dishes as the king and queen was attractive to many and Wedgwood promptly rechristened the line Queensware. He also sold a set of more than nine hundred pieces to Catherine the Great of Russia.

Wedgwood's royal endorsers were important to his success, and he was willing to sell to the Russian empress at cost because her purchase enhanced his prestige. But by Wedgwood's time, the taste-defining authority of the court had largely disappeared in England, replaced by a broader, more amorphous notion of fashionable society. This was still a small, very wealthy group. But it depended less on noble titles than on an ability to use clothing and objects in a discerning, yet imaginative way. Personalities from this time—such as Lord Chesterfield, whose letters to his son outlined a theory of quiet good taste, and Beau Brummel, who lived to dress—still influence thinking about style today. The fop—a man who was all style and no substance—was a chief figure of ridicule.

But his appearance in plays and popular literature indicates that even those who were not part of fashionable society were nevertheless interested in it.

We remember Wedgwood as one of the first marketing geniuses because of his understanding of both pottery and those who might buy it. Wedgwood's goods were made in a factory, though not by machines. He had to find products that his workers could produce with absolute consistency. He was a technical innovator, but he surrounded himself with partners and designers who paid close attention to developments in the architecture, art, and culture of his time. He quickly grasped that the simplified neoclassical designs, which were becoming popular during the late 1700s, lent themselves to factory production far better than ceramics with complicated glazes. He then began to commission artists, most notably John Flaxman, to create designs that appeared both ancient and up-to-date, and developed an efficient way to produce them.

Wedgwood shaped a taste for the product he was able to manufacture. He opened a large, elegant gallery in London, which prints from the time show as one of the finest retail spaces yet seen. Much like Ralph Lauren's store in New York's Rhinelander Mansion, Wedgwood's showroom had an aura of aristocracy and old money. And like Lauren's many products, Wedgwood's offerings were viewed as both conservative and stylish, and thus attractive to the newly wealthy who wanted to appear as if they had always been successful.

He operated much as an art dealer does today, with large, invitation-only openings attended by a glittering crowd. He created products that reflected the fashions he saw and exploited new formulations of clay and unique textures and colors that became fashions in themselves. He was particularly conscious of appealing to women, who were beginning to take a leading role in acquiring goods and decorating houses. "I need not tell you," he once wrote, "that it will be our interest to amuse and divert & please & astonish, nay, even to ravish the Ladies."

At the time, seeing what Wedgwood was doing became necessary and urgent. He created a culture around his product, and some people believed that it was important to see what he would do next. By making a fashion, he created a sense of uncertainty that helped make Wedgwood's products sell.

$\mathcal{P}$ioneers of refinement: Americans shop

Who should be respected in matters of taste and fashion has always been a more complicated question in America than elsewhere. To be an American is, in a sense, to be insecure. A country of transplants, based on democratic principles, it has no source of authority to set standards and establish taste. A handful of eighteenth-century Americans, such as owners of sprawling plantations in the South, were easily able to see themselves as the continent's aristocrats, but in many parts of the country, the leading citizens might only be the people who owned a farm somewhat larger than those of their neighbors.

The mid–eighteenth century was a prosperous time in the American colonies. Wealthy people were covering the walls of their newly built city houses and villas with cloth and filling the rooms as never before with dishes, tables, chairs, and carpets. By the eve of the Revolution, several American cities had furniture-makers and other artisans who offered goods of design and quality that were surpassed by only a handful of their counterparts in Europe.

Because the presence of objects forces those who possess them to define and understand how they are to be used, it was a period of extreme preoccupation with the issue of good manners. Etiquette is, after all, mostly about the proper use of objects. Only a few decades before, when most Americans were eating with their fingers, there was no anxiety about which fork to use.

Many successful people took it upon themselves to tackle Americans' endemic insecurity head-on and establish standards to which their countrymen could aspire. They did it by shopping. Numerous correspondences survive between women residing in rural areas and friends and relatives in Philadelphia, New York, and other regional capitals. They ask in detail how things are done by the fashionable people in the cities. They want to know how women dress for particular occasions, what kinds of meals are being served and on what sorts of dishes. Often the city correspondents are deputized as shoppers for their country friends. In this way, both hoped, civilization would be dispersed throughout the nation, and one's own status as a leader could be affirmed.

Not everyone approved of this growing material splendor. In colonial Philadelphia during the mid–eighteenth century, Benjamin Franklin, the country's greatest social entrepreneur, prospered as a young man by posing as an old man preaching thrift, austerity, and foresight. "A penny saved is a penny earned," he advised. At the time, though, the Quaker virtues of simplicity and restraint were under siege, as prosperous merchants and others, eventually including Franklin himself, built elaborate Georgian mansions. Even more worrisome, apprentice craftsmen in the city were buying garments in the latest fabrics and styles from England.

Much of the criticism of elaborate entertaining with silver-strewn tables, big houses, and big dresses came from families previously considered cultural leaders. New money always poses a threat to old money. That's because new economic opportunities produce far greater windfalls than do old riches, properly invested. Thus members of old-money families find their authority in culture and tradition. They urge restraint and satirize the superficial and vulgar ways of those whose wealth is newer and larger. "Whenever Vanity and Gaiety, a Love of Pomp and Dress, Furniture, Equipage, Buildings, great Company, expensive Diversions, and elegant Entertainments get the better of the Principles and Judgments of Men and Women," John Adams wrote, "there is no knowing where they will stop, nor into what Evils, natural, moral or political, they will lead us."

Such people frequently tame the excesses of fashion, because those with new money want to be admitted to the company of these established people and be part of the institutions they run. In the end, though, those who have the money to spend do so, and the things they buy become the authoritative objects of the next generation.

Those who sought to establish themselves as paragons of taste and refinement may have assuaged some of their own insecurities about their status and legitimacy. The effort was doomed to failure, however, because taste is about restrictions, and Americans mistrust limits. Throughout the world, aristocratic standards of taste have collapsed. As in America, fashion is what the kids say it is.

$\mathcal{C}$aring about fashion, and pretending not to

At a contemporary shopping mall, several recent studies conclude, the most fashion-conscious people you will find are females between twelve and fourteen years of age. These young people, on the cusp of womanhood, have a more detailed knowledge of the brands of products available to them, and more thoughts and questions about what the styles mean, than do members of any other age group, including the fifteen- to seventeen-year-old women, who come in second. Males in their teens claim not to pay very much attention to fashion, in part because it's not cool—fashionable, in other words—to seem to do so. But when young men are asked specific questions about brands, clothing styles, and even cosmetics, they turn out to know quite a lot after all. This pretense of being ignorant of fashion, and then being effortlessly stylish anyway, was as widespread in the eighteenth century as it is today.

The association of extreme fashion-consciousness with young adolescent females suggests a preoccupation with fitting in and being accepted by their peers. In fact, if you ask the young women, they will tell you that themselves. Today's young people are sophisticated about their motivations and about how advertisers and merchandisers try to make them behave. They become furious if they feel they are being manipulated, and contrary to what one might expect, they are not impulse-buyers. They think very carefully about their purchases, precisely because they believe them to be so important, and nowadays, they often "preshop" by checking out sites on the Internet.

The idea that at least some people shop to be part of the group seems almost self-evident. But it is a subtly different idea than the one that pervades most criticism of consumer behavior: that fashion is a matter of emulating people whose social status is higher than yours. These young women want acceptance, but by people who are in exactly the same situation as they are. It would be easier for the young women if there were accepted standards to guide them, but, especially among young people, fashion changes quickly, and large retailers have developed ways to respond to their desires in a matter of weeks. Uncertainty is endemic to adolescence. Fashion only makes that uncertainty more intense. No wonder young women feel that fitting in is hard work.

Another group highly concerned with fashion is African-American women in their twenties and thirties. They spend substantially more on clothing than do comparable non-Hispanic white women, and three out of five of them, as opposed to two out of five white women, agree that it's important to keep up with the latest styles. They are almost twice as willing to be uncomfortable in the name of style.

You might assume that African Americans, Hispanics, and Asian Americans, all of whom are more fashion-conscious than women who don't identify themselves as members of minority groups, are trying harder in order to emulate those that rank ahead of them in this culture. Based on what African-American women buy, however, members of these groups more often buy to impress one another. African-American women, shop for some items—lavish hats, for example—that white women no longer buy. Dressing up for church is still a strong tradition in predominantly African-American congregations. African-American women aren't trying to look like white women; they believe they look better.

One of the newest sources of marketers' fascination is what has been called "the role-relaxed consumer." These are people who don't appear to have any insecurity about their buying habits. They are aware of what other people are buying and wearing, but declare that they make their own consumption choices based on other standards. Some of them even devote a bit of effort to being out of style.

Studies of such people show that they tend to be affluent, well-educated, skeptical of advertising, and frequently prone to spend less than they can afford. Their watchword is not "fashion" but "value," the best quality for the money. They tell researchers that they view self-respect to be far more important than being respected by others. It seems that while affluent "role-relaxed" consumers see fashion consciousness as the opposite of self-respect, others, including African Americans, Hispanics, and Asian Americans, see being fashionable as a sincere expression of self-respect.

These role-relaxed consumer values have been adopted by many members of the baby-boomer generation. In surveys throughout the 1990s, they said they valued self-respect over winning the respect of others by a ten-to-one margin. And they indicated a much lower aspiration toward luxury hotels and other fleeting affirmations of prestige. And while it is to be expected that people would become more "role-relaxed" as they age and become more comfortable with, or resigned to, themselves, the baby boomers' conversion to these values is viewed as being far more dramatic than for any other generation.

You might think that the emergence of such a group would be the fashion-mongers' worst nightmare, but that's not quite the case. For one thing, those who are most aggressively "role-relaxed" have been found to be generators of fashion. After all, fashion depends on people doing things that are outside of the mainstream, but are then widely adopted.

In the end, though, this anti-fashion attitude is seen to be, itself, a kind of fashion, one that can generate sales. It's probably no accident that the decade of the role-relaxed consumer was also the decade of the sport-utility vehicle. A financially successful member of the boomers' parents' generation might have opted for a rather formal luxury sedan, perhaps a Cadillac or a Mercedes, to show the world they had made it. Boomers, obsessed with their own self-respect, prefer the SUV that lets them ride high above the traffic. They are secure in their own safety, oblivious to the crash threat they pose to others for whom they feel little concern. The SUVs, far from being formal, flaunt their backwoods prowess. But this macho pose may be just as symbolic, and useless, as their fathers' tailfins.

Fashion metamorphoses into all kinds of forms, from extreme dandyism to assertive neglect of one's clothing and surroundings. It can't be avoided, because just about every attempt to deny fashion turns into a fashion statement of its own. Fashion sometimes involves a measure of masochism, as the scarred bodies of tribal people and the pierced tongues and noses of contemporary young people demonstrate. But we are not slaves to fashion. Rather we shop for and use clothes and things in an always unfinished attempt to be more certain about ourselves.

ℒooking for a challenge

Still, fashion is hardly the only force that makes people buy things they don't need. In the case of my rush to loot the Wedgwood museum, for example, I was driven by an even more atavistic drive: the fear of missing out on something important.

As we have seen, the women of the Kalahari Desert, carrying children and firewood, trudge for miles through a barren landscape in search of plants, roots, or small animals their families can eat. It's easy to understand their delight at finding something they need. We live in a very different world, surrounded by all that we need and even more that we don't. There are plenty of things for people to worry about—including how they will pay the bills for their previous purchases. But compared with the Kalahari gatherer's anxiety about whether she will find enough termites to feed her family, shoppers in developed countries have it easy. Still, our shopping is motivated by the same impulse to provide for ourselves and others, and to understand that doing so still requires skill and fortitude. There needs to be something challenging about shopping, or it's not really worthwhile.

While the gatherers of the Kalahari are driven by stark human needs, contemporary shoppers are not. Yet shopping has little piquancy unless there is a possibility that we might discover something, a fear that we must act lest we lose what we have found, the hope of paying less than we expect.

Shopping is most exciting when it offers an opportunity that anyone would be foolish to forgo. This can take the form of a discovery, a rare and wonderful thing you didn't know you wanted until you saw it. Or it can be a bargain, a familiar item that is available, today only, at a much lower price than usual. It's good to be able to go to a store or log on to an online retailer and find exactly what you want at a fair price. But it doesn't compare with being able to find a treasure, or feel that you're stealing one.

There is nothing rational about such feelings. A purchase is an emotional commitment. And while manufacturers and retailers help try to shape these emotions with their advertising and display, shoppers themselves decide to define an item being offered as an opportunity that will be lost. Rationally, we know that there's plenty more where that came from, no matter what "that" happens to be. Still, we fear that we will regret it later if we don't buy when we have the chance. As shoppers, we want to find what we expect, but we may not return unless we can also find what we don't expect.

This "shoppers' uncertainty principle" is rarely discussed, but it is very real. Shoppers tell marketing researchers that what they like least is making routine purchases. Indeed, some marketers and scholars argue that the regular trip to the supermarket isn't shopping at all, simply provisioning, a completely different activity.

It's true that going to the supermarket and buying a package of Cheerios for $3.99 is not at all exciting. But that's not exactly what happens. Sometimes there's a sale and that same box of Cheerios costs $2.99. Suddenly, there is a limited opportunity, something that might compel someone for whom this item is important to make a special trip to the supermarket to stock up. Following what's promoted, clipping cents-off coupons, and seizing the opportunities for bargains makes supermarket shopping far more emotionally compelling. "Everyday low prices"—i.e., getting rid of specials and promotions—is an approach many retailers try. They can rarely do so for very long, because we shoppers won't let them make shopping dull. Promotion of bargains induces more trips to the market, during which people will purchase things that aren't on sale. One advertising study found that nine out of ten shoppers at the supermarket—men and women alike—arrive with what they feel is a strategy for saving money. They see the supermarket as a challenge to be mastered. The fear of missing out on a sale price on breakfast cereal is hardly in a class with the Kalahari gatherer's hazard of being attacked by hyenas. But it adds an element of uncertainty that helps make consumption interesting.

The same techniques are, of course, used in arenas where there is no doubt that shopping is taking place. Department stores offer one-day sales, whose promise and threat is that prices will be higher the next day, if not the next month. Outlet malls, filled with stores in which high-quality manufacturers and retailers ostensibly sold their mistakes and overruns at low prices, were among the most successful shopping centers of the affluent 1990s. Dollar stores kept pulling in profits while dot-com e-tailers were falling by the wayside, in part because such stores are unpredictable. You never know what you will find in a dollar store, only what it will cost.

Department and specialty stores also churn their inventories quickly, not just to keep up with the fast pace of fashion but to add uncertainty. Shoppers know that if they don't buy the item when they first find it, they may never be able to find it again. (There will almost certainly be something else equally attractive, but as shoppers we often choose to ignore that.)

Online retailers are grappling with the problem of how to add uncertainty to a shopping environment whose implicit promise is that everything is available. Things are changing fast in e-business, but at this point, most top online retailers have moved from very low everyday prices to a pattern of short-term and highly targeted discounts, often linked to e-mailed "coupons." This seems likely to increase both traffic and profitability. The tactic also renders price-comparison sites, whose promise is to remove all uncertainty about the lowest price, much less useful. It's a step away from the price efficiency that economists believe the Internet should foster, but it's also a step toward making shopping the Web somewhat more interesting.

It is more likely, though, that the promise of universal availability of products on the Internet is changing the way people shop, at least for some goods, both on the Web and in actual stores. I used to buy more books before Amazon.com and its competitors revolutionized bookselling. That's because when I was browsing a bookstore and found a book that looked interesting, I frequently bought it immediately for fear that I might not find it again. Now that I can always get it online, I often delay the purchase. But once the initial passion has passed, I rarely follow through.

I can't point to any data that indicates my behavior is typical, though it is clear that online retailing has not expanded the market for most products. But my response does point to some things about e-shopping that are fairly obvious. One is that the Web is a terrible place to browse through large numbers of items to discover the one thing you didn't know you wanted. The Web, by contrast, is unequaled for finding the best price for a particular item you know you want. But the promise of certainty on the Internet works against what the store offers: the possibility of discovery, combined with a pressure to buy that comes from uncertainty that you will be able to find the item again.

It may seem perverse to argue that the Internet, which offers more people more information than they have ever had before, needs a dose of uncertainty. Yet consider eBay, the first great business success of the Internet. This is a vast flea market. You don't know what you'll find there, but it's close to certain that if you look carefully, you'll find something quite interesting. Electronically rummaging through eBay is like rooting through the dusty merchandise of a secondhand-seller's booth, and you keep going because the treasure may be just one layer deeper. Then, once you find the treasure, you don't know whether you'll be able to buy it. You have to bid on it, and you may lose. You come back to the site again and again to see how you are doing, and you may well rummage some more.

The lesson of eBay is that it combines the richness of information and large communities available on the 'Net with the uncertainty of the bargain hunter and auction buyer. The Web marketers' term for sites whose users return frequently and spend long periods of time is "sticky." On eBay at least, uncertainty is what makes shoppers stick.

$\mathcal{S}$hopping as sickness

Conspiring with retailers to conjure up uncertainties to overcome and challenges to meet is a harmless game. For some people, though, insecurities can become too great, and shopping becomes a means not of self-enhancement but of self-destruction.

Problem shoppers appear to have many of the same psychological characteristics as compulsive gamblers. Both shopping and gambling are ways of adding excitement and surprise to life. They offer the hope of sudden, unpredictable transformation.

There is no consensus about what percentage of the population are problem shoppers, or even whether problem shopping is an illness in itself, a symptom of other problems, or just everyday behavior that has somehow gotten out of control. Those who can pay their bills are viewed as good customers; only those in debt are seen to have problems.

Those who have studied problem shoppers have found that about one in ten is a man, likely to go on sprees of purchasing electronics equipment and do-it-yourself items associated with masculinity and competence. The great majority of "shopaholics" are women, who tend to buy jewelry, clothing, and cosmetics, in the hope, they report, that if they look better they will feel better. According to a profile created by researchers at Stanford, based on about two dozen heavily indebted shoppers, problem shoppers report "blanking out" in the store and claim they had no awareness of what they were doing. They report a release of tension after buying, followed by feelings of guilt, anger, and sadness. Once they get the items home, they often fail to remove them from their packages or cut off the tags. Some return their purchases, but more hide them.

Lorrin Koran, the psychiatrist who conducted the Stanford study, believes that problem shopping is a result of anxiety and depression, and he believes in treating the problem with anti-depressant drugs. Pharmaceutical companies have funded research on problem shopping, presumably because they hope that once it is officially accepted as a form of mental illness, it will provide a new market for their products. Other studies have concluded that drugs are not effective. Many psychiatrists prefer to see problem shopping as a characteristically female way to cope with feelings of emptiness rooted in poor self-esteem, a sense of being neglected, or an unsatisfactory sex life. And some problem shoppers appear to spend themselves into debt semideliberately, in order to provoke a financial crisis in a marriage or relationship with which they are dissatisfied.

The most troubling thing about the literature on problem shopping is how closely it seems to resemble behavior and feelings that most shoppers would consider normal. One study argues that addictive shoppers are driven by the fear of missing out, just as most other shoppers are. Another argues that purchasing something without either a plan or a specific need is itself evidence of pathology. Still, everyone who has ever gone shopping has sometimes come home, looked at a purchase, and wondered, "What was I thinking?" In retrospect, it often seems that you weren't thinking at all, that you were simply caught up in a mania of acquisition. In some cases, you might return the purchase (though you might be required to pick out something else to replace it). Retailers have succeeded in making any individual purchase seem to be unimportant. Sales are quick, credit is easy. You needn't give the thing a second thought. And often you don't, even if you can't afford it.

In a 2000 study, 36 percent of women and 18 percent of men admitted buying things they didn't need. About one woman in four says she "can't resist a sale," and about one in three women shop to celebrate. Retail therapy, or compensatory consumption, as most scholars label it, is an extremely common practice. Many food products, for example, are marketed as small rewards that provide a momentary escape from life's demands. Premium coffee is explicitly marketed to women, with messages and imagery shaped by study of their fantasies of escape.

"Usually I buy something that I feel guilty about, just something that I've probably got three or four of at home," a forty-five-year-old married English nurse told psychologist Helen R. Woodruffe in a 1997 article on compensatory consumption. "I'm not an extravagant shopper—just some little thing, I suppose, to try and lift your spirits. Bargains are also important and good for mood repair: If I get a good reduction—if I know I've got a bargain—even if I don't really want it—if I know I've got a good bargain—it raises you a bit." Every one of these emotions is part of the classic profile of the problem shopper. But because she is able to keep her impulses under control, she is studied not as a sick person, but as a fairly typical one.

Throughout the book, I have been arguing that shopping is an exercise of both profound responsibility and profound freedom. But there is no doubt that it can also serve as an escape from responsibility and as a substitute for meaningful action. Insecurity is the price of living in a society that believes in self-creation, openness, and change. Our insecurities leave us open to psychological manipulation, which in turn helps keep the economic engine running.

These two visions of the shopper—as hero and as dupe—seem irreconcilable yet true. The only way to resolve this paradox is to recognize that most of the time most people choose to allow themselves to be manipulated. They conspire in their own seduction. It can be enjoyable to do so, but, as the existence of problem shoppers reminds us, also hazardous. It is, of course, possible to overdo anything, and shoppers are constantly being tempted to overindulge. And there is danger in the popular adage that the person who dies with the most toys wins, which often serves as a justification for men's shopping sprees. Winning a game like that can lead to an overcrowded house and an empty life. Shoppers may sometimes be victimized, but we need not be victims. By keeping our insecurities under control, we can learn to resist yet appreciate that we are free to buy.

6
ATTENTION

Sellers, Buyers, and the Worlds They Make

a friend I'll call Phil had just bought a new book and was really excited. Because Phil is both an avid reader and a collector of books, it was difficult at first to understand his enthusiasm for this particular purchase. Quickly, though, it became obvious that what made this book special was the way it had been sold to him.

Phil had not seen the book or been aware of it in any way until he received an e-mail from an online retailer. It told him that, based on his previous purchases, he might be interested in a book that had recently become available. In addition, it said, because he was such a good customer, he would be offered a price lower than that for which the book was listed online.

What was interesting about this solicitation was that he didn't recall any past purchases that would make it obvious to either a person or a computer that he would want this book. It was not, for example, by an author whose work he had ordered before, or part of a series of titles. Nevertheless, it was a book he wanted very much indeed. He hit the e-mail link, so he could get his special price, ordered immediately, and three days later, it was in his hands.

The Internet seller had paid attention to Phil and, as a consequence, it had helped Phil satisfy a desire of which he hadn't been aware. Sellers have always known that shoppers crave attention. They want their desires to be recognized, their tastes to be flattered, and their eyes to be opened. They want to be surprised and delighted and to feel that they are important.

Paying attention to the customer is essential, but it must be the right kind of attention. Shopping is, in part, an exercise of freedom. Thus the attention the merchant pays cannot be intrusive. It cannot be judgmental. Usually the best way to pay attention to shoppers is to stay out of their way unless they ask for help. Great store displays, beautiful buildings, and even good packaging can be very effective ways of paying attention to the shopper. Throughout the nineteenth century, great retailers invented techniques to liberate shoppers and serve them. Now the Internet is opening new possibilities for paying the right kind of attention to shoppers.

Phil's purchase had been made possible by computer software that can find patterns in a person's purchases and collate them with the buying habits of others. The premise is that you will like products bought by those who show a buying profile similar to yours. What makes this technology interesting is that the patterns that emerge do not conform to what most people would consider to be sensible categories. Assume, for example, that you have bought three blue Oxford-cloth button-down shirts, a water filter, a Duke Ellington box set, a stock pot, three books on school reform, and a dozen candles. The software compares it with others who exhibit similar behavior, and it might conclude that you want a streamlined toaster with extra-wide slots to accommodate English muffins, or a sweater hand-knitted in Bolivia by Incas. And if it has enough information from you and countless others, it will very likely be right.

For most people, these systems don't yet work very well because they haven't supplied enough data to allow the software to jump to any interesting conclusions. The recommendations are, more often than not, simple-minded. Very likely, you ordered those items from several different merchants, one of whom thinks you buy only shirts; another, only jazz; a third, only books on school reform; and the result is boring recommendations. But Phil, a frequent buyer at the same site, has apparently provided enough data to enable the computer to surprise him. I have to confess that it surprised me. I have known Phil for years, but would never have dared recommend this book.

It was, you see, a book of erotic drawings. Technically, they were superb, but the fantasies they depicted were, most people would probably agree, borderline kinky. This was a book that probably wouldn't be stocked by any store in the small city where Phil lives, and if it were, probably would not be on display. A year or two ago, Phil said, it would have been unlikely that he would have found the book, much less feel comfortable buying it.

I agreed, though less than wholeheartedly. I have no idea what else Phil might have ordered to induce the computer to make so appropriate a recommendation. But I am not at all certain that I would want insight into my strongest, strangest, most private desires available on the Internet, ripe for exploitation. Phil countered that most of this same information can be discerned from credit card records. If he had tried to buy this book where he lived and was well known, he added, someone might have noticed and disapproved. If he were hoping for appointment to the Supreme Court, Phil said, he might feel otherwise, but he viewed this transaction to be relatively private.

I could see his point, and I can certainly see that the technology that sent him the book has the potential for replacing the kind of expert help and thoughtful salesmanship that has largely disappeared from the retail experience in recent years. For Phil it provided a fully satisfactory shopping experience, and as all of us build up richer databases of our tastes, desires, pretenses, and weaknesses, there is little doubt that there will be pleasant shopping surprises ahead.

Yet, unlike some of the people shown in Phil's picture book, I am not quite ready to surrender myself completely. As I thumbed through the pages, I resolved, then and there, to continue to do my online shopping at a variety of sites, lest the computer identify some perversion I don't even know I have.

What Phil considers to be a very useful kind of attention, I view as a breach of my privacy.

Privacy may seem an odd concept when discussing shopping. Buying things may be an intimate act, but, at least until recently, it has been done in a public setting. We are rarely able to be wholly alone with our desires. Shopping involves other people: salesclerks, friends, fellow shoppers, passersby. And as long as there have been stores and people have been going to stores, there has been a tension between shoppers' needs for information, assistance, and reassurance, and their reluctance to be judged by others and have their business known.

Shopping is, in large part, about finding and refining identity. That means that the shopper is, like a crab that has just shed an old shell, uniquely vulnerable. Thus we like to have friends with us to give permission and tell us that we're making the right choice. We also like, at least some of the time, to have a well-informed salesclerk point out advantages and alternatives and to hold our hand until the sale is made. Indeed, some theorize that the reason so many Internet sales are abandoned almost at the end is that there is nobody there—not even a cashier—to keep us company during those crucial moments of committing to a purchase.

Yet the presence of others inevitably adds an emotional dimension to shopping that can easily get in the way of making a purchase. A fleeting grimace on the face of a friend, or a clerk whose manner seems condescending rather than helpful, can kill the desire to buy. Retailers can't do a thing about friends, except make them feel welcome and comfortable about granting the permission to buy.

They can, however, fine-tune the way in which they sell, so that shoppers feel that they are getting the right kind of attention. Shoppers want attention that is personal, discreet, understanding, and nonjudgmental, which is a difficult combination to achieve. For most of the last two centuries, nearly every change in the buyosphere has tended to suppress the expression of the seller's personality, and to support and encourage the desires of the buyer. In a sense, then, shopping has become increasingly impersonal. The great retailers have accelerated shopping by reducing the emotional friction between seller and buyer.

Such innovations as fixed and marked prices, open display, large department stores, ready-to-wear clothing, informative and evocative packaging, self-service, and electronic scanners have all reduced the amount of human interaction involved in making a purchase. The sophisticated technology that identified Phil's desires and sold him the book is a logical extension of this long-term trend. Shopping is still as emotional an act as ever, but it is less likely to be derailed by the friction that can develop when the shopper simply doesn't hit it off with the salesclerk.

A lady shops: Negotiating for a dress

Though today's shoppers often complain about getting too little attention, during the early nineteenth century, shoppers received so much attention that buying a length of fabric could turn into an emotional ordeal. Certainly the shopping experience was very different in 1844, when *Godey's Ladies Book*, the pioneering U.S. women's magazine, published this vignette about a woman shopper who loved a bargain:

> "What is the price of this material?" I asked of a very assiduous young gentleman, as I was passing out of a dry-goods store . . .
>
> "Indeed?" said I; and "Indeed!" I repeated more emphatically, when he named the price—for it really seemed low beyond precedent.
>
> "You will allow me to cut you off a dress, will you not?" said he.
>
> "Oh, no; I merely asked the price through curiosity;—I am in no need of the article."
>
> "But you certainly could make use of it; almost any lady might have occasion for such a dress—and even if you should not, there would be little cause to regret having purchased it. Remember

what a trifle it would amount to. Pray, let me persuade you, miss."

"I believe not; the colors are rather light for a winter dress," I replied.

"But they will admirably suit the approaching season; and I cannot—I beg pardon, miss—agree with you that they are too delicate to be worn at the present time . . ."

"You really should have a dress of it," he added, with the kindest solicitude; "and to have the pleasure of supplying you with one, I would go so far as to put it a third lower. Do gratify me, miss."

This really seemed an extraordinary bargain, and, besides, if I must confess the whole truth, I was considerably mollified in my resolution not to buy what I did not want by being waited on so gallantly, and so confidently addressed by the monosyllabic title, an indirect attestation to the youthfulness of my appearance very flattering to one who stood within three years of thirty; so I requested that the usual quantity might be cut off for me.

"Might it not be as well to take two or three yards more, to makeup full, it is so cheap?" said the salesman, with the thoughtful prudence of one deeply versed in the political economy of a lady's wardrobe; and I agreed that it might be as well to take two or three yards more.

When the salesman "cut her off a dress," which meant, at the time, enough material to make a dress, the labor of getting something new to wear was only beginning. As the story continues, the narrator goes next to a dressmaker, who convinces her to make a very elaborate dress, since the material is so cheap, and then to another dry-goods store to purchase buttons, ribbons, and trimming to deliver to the dressmaker. (The point of the story is that what seems to be a bargain can turn into an extravagance.)

The reason I have quoted the story so extensively, though, is to point out the emotional labor involved in buying a length of cloth. This was, at once, a tough negotiation over price, and also a kind of flirtation. The shopper feigns disinterest, and looks for things about which to complain. The salesman in turn must find ways to flatter the customer without appearing to do so. He also manages to increase her total purchase, even as he ostensibly surrenders to her on price. While the woman in the story is depicted as enjoying the transaction, it consumes so much of her energy and intellect that she is not likely to purchase things in the casual, almost inattentive way that people buy today. She has received plenty of attention, but from the store's point of view, and even from the buyer's, the attention wasn't entirely useful.

The rise of the woman shopper and the feminized buyosphere

Arguably the most important new phenomenon we find in the *Godey's* story is the female narrator, the shopper herself. Shopping is presented in the story as a feminine pursuit, perhaps the chief feminine pursuit. A distinct woman's world was emerging, of which *Godey's*, the magazine that printed the story, was both a symptom and a promoter. And when the genteel but lively women who populated its stories left their homes, more often than not, they said they were "going shopping."

During the eighteenth century, shopping was as much a province of men as of women, and it was commonly assumed that young women, at least, would be chaperoned when they went out to the stores. Already in some eighteenth-century novels, we see women shopping together, and sometimes going to stores simply to look at items they had no intention of buying. Much of the time, though, such window-shopping, which is so commonplace now, is depicted as at best a vulgar pastime and at worst a sort of perversion that could place women in harm's way.

In the nineteenth century, spending time in the shops was transformed from an indulgence for women to a duty. The retail shops themselves were no longer adjuncts to workshops but rather were places solely intended to encourage purchases. And the mood of these shops was set by the need to pay special attention to women, who had become the chief buyers.

This new women's world emerged in the cities of virtually all industrializing countries during the first third of the nineteenth century, and it was part of a radical change in the economics of the household. Wives and children were no longer productive members of the family business, learning it and able to take it over if necessary. They lived behind many layers of draperies in a domestic refuge, sheltered from the world of work. Children of moderately prosperous families were expected to spend increasing amounts of their lives being educated and preparing to survive in a world that was increasingly unpredictable. The wife had the chief duty to guide and nurture this next generation, and to create a household that embodied the cultural and material achievements of the family.

In America, this idea began to flourish during the 1830s, just about the time that Italianate domestic architecture began to take hold. That's why, in New York, the brownstone buildings that first appeared at that moment remain, even today, the very image of bourgeois respectability. Other cities, such as Philadelphia and Boston, used more brick than brownstone, but these houses, plainer but infinitely more numerous than their elite predecessors, mark a major change in city life.

Like all change—even that which brings an apparent improvement of fortune—this new way of life provoked great anxiety. The lady of the house worried not only about whether the things she bought would make a good impression on others, but also whether her husband would deem her purchases appropriate and economical. Shopping was one of the chief ways she could prove she was paying attention to the needs of her family.

There is little doubt that husbands were worried, for along with the emergence of women as household managers came the stereotype of women as wild spenders and destroyers of fortunes. Calling the woman "the angel of the household" ascribed to females a quasi-religious authority, one that is consistent with the idea that shopping is a form of sacrifice. But when the man of the house allowed his wife to become priestess of consumption, he feared that he was giving up power, losing control of all he had produced. Often, this was more psychological than real, because in many places at the time, a married woman could incur debts only on behalf of her husband who did, in fact, have the final say about what was bought. But Adam had had the last word, too, and look what happened to him.

Men showed particular concern that clerks in the shops might lead women astray. They worried that fast-talking salesmen would convince their wives to buy more than they needed, but even more than that, men feared the feminine world of the shopper and mistrusted the men who made their living there.

The retail salesman of the first half of the nineteenth century was a professional of sorts, formally dressed and generally well-spoken, with some education. Store proprietors placed a great deal of trust in their salesmen, because it was they who often determined at what price an item would be sold. This created an anxiety for proprietors parallel to the one felt by husbands: Were their employees giving away the store?

Drawings of American stores of the period typically depict fabric salesmen as young, wearing tailcoats and very tight pants. They stood behind mahogany or walnut counters on which they skillfully draped fabrics in what was seen to be a very tempting way. There were chairs on the customer's side of the counter, for a purchase could be a leisurely and time-consuming process. But there were no chairs on the salesman's side, because store owners hated to see them sit down.

Despite their fine manners and fine clothes, the salesmen were not wholly respectable characters. "They remind you of loungers about theaters," another *Godey's* writer observed. Knowing so much about cloth and dresses was not seen as a wholly masculine attribute, and nearly everything written about salesmen during this period contains some innuendo about their sexuality.

The stereotype of the effeminate salesman is, in fact, so pronounced, that it very likely speaks to a common anxiety rather than to a literal truth. Since the selling of goods was frequently seen as a form of seduction, perhaps it was reassuring for husbands to assume that the young men wooing their wives to buy were not the sort of men who would have any sexual interest in them.

"Some of the young gentlemen, in truth, are *not so* very delightful," wrote an anonymous woman in New York's *Harper's Weekly* in 1858, echoing a common complaint. "Some of them are very *conceited, supercilious,* and *unsatisfactory.* Perhaps we who are not very young tend to be a little more exacting; but I do not like to be treated as if I were having a favor conferred on me by a young man in a shop when he shows me goods." She had a radical suggestion: saleswomen. While dresses were not sold ready to wear at the time, undergarments were, and she said she had no desire to have a young man showing such things to her daughter.

The woman was speaking of A. T. Stewart's store, the so-called marble palace, which opened in New York in 1846. It was far and away the largest, most luxurious store America had ever seen. Stewart's store was the chief cause of what *Harper's Weekly* termed "the dry goods epidemic," a malady whose symptom was an extreme curiosity about the latest fashions and a willingness to crowd into the store at the beginning of the season when the newest lines arrived.

Shops had long since stopped being quiet places. Indeed, they were increasingly frantic. One senses in accounts of browsing and buying during this period a mania that seems wholly modern.

Moreover, this mania was not restricted to the elite. There were still a few stores in most major cities where the lady would wait in her carriage while the owner of the shop would rush out with samples for her approval. But by the early nineteenth century, this drive-in approach had given way to large establishments and the places known as bazaars. These were precursors to today's shopping malls, in which dozens of small shops were gathered under a single roof in a warren of arcades. They still wanted customers who owned carriages, because they were big spenders. But now the merchants started to provide places where the carriage could wait while the lady came in and looked for herself.

Many merchants, including those whose stores grew into the first department stores, built palatial establishments that sought to convince their shoppers that they were entering a magical and privileged realm. Simply walking through such places was a memorable experience for their shoppers, one that people viewed as fashionable and luxurious. People spoke of them as palaces, though their real innovation was as places where many different strata of society felt comfortable shopping together. People perceived these stores as "exclusive," though secret of their success lay in their inclusiveness. What they provided was luxury, but it was something new, a popular luxury.

During the first half of the nineteenth century, some retailers followed an entirely different approach than did the proprietors of the dry goods palaces. These merchants made a very good living without even the pretense of catering to the carriage trade. Many of them offered goods at what were generally deemed to be low, fixed prices for cash. There was no elegance in these stores, no pretense of cultivation. Often the goods sold were simply piled on the sidewalk outside the store. They followed the philosophy that became known, in the twentieth century, as "pile it high, sell it low." At the time, such businesses were known as "fast sellers," and speed was the point. Each purchase was discrete. It wasn't part of an ongoing relationship in which the seller needed to judge the buyer's creditworthiness and personal wealth.

These fast sellers were obvious precursors to today's discount and outlet stores. Less obviously, they paved the way for nearly all the retailers of the late nineteenth century, including the great department stores, and for all shopping since. Their great innovation was to shift the focus of commerce from the human transaction to the goods being bought. In other stores, price was contingent upon an often genteel but emotionally complex negotiation between buyer and seller. The fast sellers allowed shoppers to make quick judgments without being judged in return.

Buying in quantity to meet new needs

Buying quickly means buying more. The lesson of the fast sellers quickly trickled up to the higher-class merchants, who realized that they could not afford to put so much labor into selling a few yards of cloth, especially when the factories were producing goods in greater quantities than the world had ever known. In order to sell more, they had to pay attention to new ways in which the goods they offered could be made part of the rituals of daily life. In other words, they had to change how people lived.

During the early nineteenth century, the industrial manufacture of cloth and, later, of other goods, spread from England to America and throughout Europe. Mechanized textile manufacture had changed even the definition of luxury. Earlier, garments had been designed to show off the quality of the cloth. During the nineteenth century, following a short-lived vogue for skimpy, rather revealing women's clothing inspired by that of ancient Greece, fashions tended to revel in quantity, not necessarily quality. In addition, petticoats and other undergarments proliferated, using up still more of the increasingly affordable cloth. The Victorian lady routinely wore far more yards of material than anyone who had ever lived, and, eventually, the thought of wearing less seemed scandalous. She enjoyed her new freedom to go shopping, but she had to wrap herself in layers of clothes to do so.

The easy availability of cloth in quantity helped change many social practices. One of the strangest and most pervasive was the etiquette of mourning. Paying proper attention to the beloved dead found its most elaborate expression in England, but this practice was also important to a lesser degree in the United States and in other European countries. There were degrees of mourning, which depended both on who had died and the closeness of one's relationship to the deceased. Mourning could go on for weeks or months, which, for many, required the acquisition of an entire second wardrobe to show proper respect. Shops that sold black cloth and other accoutrements of mourning positioned themselves as educators and arbiters of protocol, and throughout the century, the practices became more complex and expensive. (Queen Victoria's protracted mourning of Prince Albert also had a strong influence.)

One hesitates to argue that behavior that encouraged such effusive and seemingly sincere outpourings of emotion was a product of the availability of inexpensive cloth. Yet it had not happened before, and it is scarcely conceivable that people would have been able to acquire so much black bombazine a century earlier, when textiles were still very expensive.

Just as cheaper cloth had remade women's wardrobes, so, too, did it help shape the interiors of their houses. By midcentury, the entire house was draped and upholstered. There were curtains, on the windows, and curtains to frame the curtains and swags to crown the window. And while upholstered, cushioned chairs had previously been a rarity, now almost every room had them. These consumed more yards of textiles, and more hours for the lady of the house to choose and acquire these goods. In addition, a vastly larger percentage of the population was living this new, softer, more comfortable life. Grandchildren of people who had made do with a chair or two, some pewter plates, a few glasses, and a table, now lived overfurnished lives.

In all aspects of life, specialized goods were being created to help consumers pay proper attention to the increasingly elaborate rituals of domesticity and hospitality. Setting a proper table required a huge inventory of plates, serving pieces, cutlery, and glassware. Silversmiths, for example, began to produce specialized implements for almost anything one might eat. Fish required a particular knife and fork, bouillon had its spoon, asparagus its tongs, and oysters a whole array of apparatus. And each beverage acquired its own kind of glass, and different wines demanded different shapes. Clutter, which had previously been a luxury only the rich could afford, had become close to unavoidable for that substantial middle-class minority. Life was filling up with stuff. Most of it was sold not by fast-talking salesmen but by changing expectations of what was required to prove yourself a good wife and a good hostess.

Big cities, big stores, and the thrill of anonymity

Sometimes the most exciting kind of attention is none at all. Retailing has profited mightily from one of the most potent inventions of the nineteenth century: anonymity. Getting lost amid strangers frees you from what others know and expect of you. It allows you to imagine being a different person. It invites you to wonder about the others in the crowd, and what they are thinking and dreaming. Being unknown offers a delicious freedom, the possibility that you can turn yourself into someone unexpected and surprising. All of these feelings encourage shopping. Retailers learned during the late nineteenth century how to pay attention while pretending not to. By doing so, they gave their customers the freedom to buy more.

Both in Europe and America, the largest cities sprawled across the landscape and attracted hundreds of thousands of new inhabitants. Horse-drawn omnibuses helped spawn one ring of suburbs, then steam railroads and subway systems spawned others, all of which became part of the new larger city of strangers. In America, the potent combination of industrialization and immigration made cities like New York, Philadelphia, Boston, and Chicago double and redouble in size in a matter of decades. In Europe, ancient cities such as London and Paris exploded to many times their previous size. The city of beggars and plutocrats, clerks and pickpockets, innocents and reprobates inspired both fear and fascination. Getting lost in the big city could bring either ruin or revelation. One fact was certain, though: It wouldn't be dull.

Throughout the century, as the cities burgeoned, the stores mirrored the cities of which they were a part. They became places in which one could become benignly lost, while finding both yourself and several things to buy besides.

Early in the nineteenth century, Paris had replaced London as the world's chief shopping city, the capital of style and the heart of retail innovation. Many of the luxury businesses that had served the royal court now appealed, very successfully, to a wider public with fine craftsmanship and bold design. And Paris dominated its country even more strongly than London did; everyone with any ambition had to go there, and to be outfitted with the kind of clothes and possessions that would make an impression in that most exacting of cities.

The grandest shops of Paris specialized in *nouveautés*, a word whose full impact isn't conveyed by the literal translation "novelties," or by the American retail term, "notions," which nowadays refers to buttons and such. These shops did deal in buttons and ribbons, along with a wide array of other sorts of decorations, but what they really promised was the new. These fashions were based not on aristocratic styles but on bold acts of imagination. Obviously, the upper class was important; somebody had to buy the expensive fashions. But the styles themselves were not simply expressions of taste. They were, rather, attempts to redefine taste.

Parisian retail establishments themselves were rapidly becoming a wonder of the world. "Once we had shops filled with pretty things," wrote a *Godey's* correspondent from Paris in 1844. "[T]hen we had stores; now the stores are changed into immense bazaars, upon entering which, you may imagine a whole town of curiosities to lie before you. On the ground floor, spacious apartments, ornamented with splendor . . . mirrors on all sides, a painted and waxed floor, and magnificent carpets. You imagine yourself deceived, you fancy yourself in the gallery at Versailles, and would not dare to ask for a small quantity of flannel . . . in such a palace, if it were not that you perceive a world of clerks and shop boys, coming and going, folding and unfolding, measuring shawls, and selling scarfs, silks, cravats! and a crowd of people of all classes, looking, admiring and buying."

It's worth noting that this description was written more than a decade before Paris got its first department store. Yet much of what we assume was wholly new about department stores—the mixing of classes, the theatricality, the opulence that excited a sense of being privileged and the bustle that made the shopper feel like an anonymous observer—is already apparent in this account.

The willingness to leave shoppers alone, to let them wander and discover things for themselves, did not come naturally to merchants. Indeed, London, which had been for centuries the greatest shopping city in the world, fell behind Paris, several American cities, and even some provincial cities of England, precisely because merchants there were unwilling to let the shopper roam free.

Throughout the entire Victorian era, London's stores were still operated in a very paternalistic way. William Whitely, probably the most innovative London retailer of the mid-nineteenth century, styled himself as "the universal provider," and his pretense was that he looked out for his customers' moral welfare as well as their material needs. He helped make shopping a safe and respectable activity for unaccompanied women by installing genteel lavatory facilities and sitting rooms for them. His employees, like most retail workers in London but not elsewhere, lived in company dormitories, and were encouraged to think of themselves as an extended family that provided a safe and wholesome shopping experience. Whitely's store opened to London's women a new universe of buying possibilities, and it helped create a distinctly feminine buyosphere. Nevertheless, the service and protection it offered communicated that women were uniquely imperiled and that they needed to be protected both from unscrupulous men and from their own weakness and folly.

It's possible that London ladies required greater reassurance of gentility than did their Paris or New York counterparts, though they showed themselves willing to let themselves be jostled and climbed over by fellow passengers on the omnibuses they rode to Whitely's suburban store. London merchants displayed a degree of attentiveness that was designed to scare away those who did not move immediately to at least show interest in buying something specific. Store clerks were trained to show no impatience if a shopper asked to see one item, then another, then yet another, without actually buying. But the shopper who came through the doors with nothing specific in mind, and claimed to be just looking, discouraging active sales assistance, was made to feel distinctly unwelcome, especially if she wasn't known to the store clerks.

Shopping was growing explosively in both Europe and America, but there were cultural differences in the way it was understood. In England, the issue was control. The press showed great concern both about the dangers shoppers faced in navigating the city unescorted, and of the temptations they would face, not only from store clerks but from men who might seek to entice them sexually. One of the most important ways of protecting women was to make sure that they weren't exposed to "the wrong sort," which meant that a lot of people who did not appear to be of the proper class were shown the door.

In France, the issue was not so much class as standards. The woman was more likely to be celebrated as the upholder of the nation's superior taste. She was not viewed as the target for merchants; she was their collaborator in the creation of style. While London stores were conceived as an aggregation of salesclerks and their customers, Paris stores increasingly presented a world of possibilities the shopper could afford, or even expand.

American retailers, uneasy with both rigid class distinctions of the English and arbitrary taste standards of the French, successfully appealed to the snobbery of the masses. They welcomed a broad section of the populace into stores that were calibrated to be a little bit finer than the shoppers suspected they deserved, then worked to assuage the social insecurities of those who had the money to pay the price. The woman shopper, feared though she was, was seen to be exercising, if sometimes misguidedly, the freedom that was her birthright.

Thus, the French and American store owners understood that it was in their interest to allow shoppers to drift through their stores, as through a dream. In Paris, journalists and retailers made note of a new kind of woman, the *palpeuse,* or "caresser." She moved through the store, touching everything and buying little or nothing. Some observers saw this as a form of insanity or sexual perversion, or as yet another modern menace. Unlike in London, though, retailers in Paris (and in most American cities) made life easy for the *palpeuse* by filling the store with enticing things to see and touch. They understood that this sensual experience was an important part of what they offered, and that desires are not always expressed in words. Increasingly, clerks and managers were instructed not to speak to shoppers unless spoken to or signaled. The merchants understood that the wandering shopper might find something she did not think to ask for. And even if a shopper did not make a purchase every time, if the store had provided an environment where the shopper felt both comfortable and stimulated, she would return when she did have a purchase to make. Giving her a magical place and leaving her alone to experience it was just the sort of attention she needed.

Fixing the price, freeing the shopper

The transformation of stores from places where you went to purchase a specific item to theaters for exploring your desires made a big difference in their physical form. Stores made more space for highly dramatic display, and for a very broad selection of merchandise. Mahogany counters and tight-packed shelves gave way to glass cases. These could serve as counters, but their main advantage was that they allowed solitary perusal of items without the intervention of any clerk. This aim was apparent in the name of the leading American manufacturer of these items: The Phillips Silent Salesman Showcase Co.

It was inevitable that as display became more important stores would become larger. One reason is obvious: Display takes up more space. A more important reason, though, is that shoppers themselves changed their perceptions. The already tenuous connection between the workshop where goods were made and the retail shop where they were bought was severed at last. The best shops were not necessarily those with a particular expertise. Rather, they were the best places for shopping, the ones with the best displays, the most attractive goods, and the most helpful, but not intrusive, staff.

Thus it was easy to imagine buying cloth for draperies, a leather belt, stockings and perfume from a single store.

The changing role of the sales staff also encouraged growth. No longer was each sale the result of an emotionally fraught negotiation. Increasingly, shoppers went to stores not to be sold to, but to select from the store's offerings, and the salesman presented himself as a helpful bystander and representative of a larger entity. The reputation of the store itself, along with the experience it offered, outweighed the influence of any individual salesperson. In this sort of store, haggling over price was clearly inappropriate. Fixed and marked prices gave shoppers a greater sense of being in control of their destinies. Not incidentally, they gave the store owners greater control as well. Fixed prices, by simplifying the management of the store and reducing the trust placed in salesmen, made it easier for stores to expand.

For shoppers, having the price marked was even more important than having it fixed. These grand stores were new sorts of places where people weren't entirely certain how to behave. They didn't want to risk the embarrassment of asking about an item they could not possibly afford. The price tag reduced some of the social risk of shopping, and thus increased the total number of shoppers.

Fixed prices became common in Paris earlier than in most other major cities, and it is no accident that stores there expanded more quickly than elsewhere. For the first time, shoppers expected stores to occupy several floors of a large building, complete with grand staircases for promenading, and open balconies, from which cloth could be draped. A. T. Stewart's marble palace was a conscious imitation of a Paris-type store, complete with the grand staircase and fixed prices. Indeed, Stewart's prices were as low as the setting was lavish, an extremely seductive combination.

Nearly all the great department stores started out as cloth merchants. (London's Harrod's, which began as a grocer, is the chief exception.) In cities throughout Europe and America successful retailers kept adding one line after another, keeping and expanding the ones that worked while discarding others. Little by little, without quite meaning to, they invented the department store, a place to shop that was more than the sum of its parts. In 1859, it all came together in Paris when Aristide Boucicaut opened the first building that was designed as this new kind of store, the first of the *grands magasins* ("big stores"). It was named not for its proprietor but for the innovation that made it possible: *Le Bon Marché,* "the good price."

*R*eady-to-wear: Exploding choices, expanding stores

Perhaps the most important retailing innovation of the century—the one that transformed drapers' shops into great department stores—was the introduction of ready-to-wear clothing. As we have seen, there had long been markets in used clothing, and by the early nineteenth century, underwear and a few other items were commonly produced ready-to-wear. But up until that time, tailoring clothing had been viewed as so complicated a task that there was little point in doing it for an imaginary wearer. Each piece of clothing was made for a particular person, to the measurements of his or her body.

Retailing lore recounts that the first merchant ever to sell a ready-made suit was Henry Sands Brooks, founder, in 1818, of Brooks Brothers. The reason he gave was that many of his customers were sea captains who didn't have time to wait for a custom-made suit, though they were usually ashore long enough for alterations to be done to a garment on which the most time-consuming tailoring had been completed. In retrospect, this was a revolutionary change, though it didn't seem so to Brooks, who saw it as a relatively minor part of his business.

What was required was a change in the way people thought about their clothes. For most people in the early nineteenth century, buying a suit or a dress was a major project. Involving as it did the choice of fabric, buttons, and countless nuances of style, as well as negotiations with suppliers and with a tailor or dressmaker, it was a complex operation. It was not quite as unnerving as adding a room to your house, perhaps, but it was a lot harder than a modern-day trip to the mall. And the toughest part of it was knowing what you wanted ahead of time.

Increasingly, items such as furniture, clocks, and guns, which had previously been crafted by artisans from start to finish, were being made in factories by less skilled workers, each of whom performed only part of the task. Doing the same with tailoring and dressmaking was not a large conceptual leap, but it was, nevertheless, slow in coming. Clothes, which were made for specific bodies, did not seem so amenable to standardization. Clothes were seen more as a problem to be solved than as a possibility to be considered. Retailers hesitated to offer ready-to-wear clothing because they guessed, correctly, that much of it would remain unsold. They didn't realize that by offering ready-to-wear goods, they could sell more garments, for profits that would more than compensate for the goods they didn't sell.

Many retailers did, however, understand the benefit of making up some finished garments as display samples, so that shoppers could see what they might do with the cloth and trimmings. Many shoppers, not surprisingly, wanted items exactly like those on display. Clearly, it is easier to choose from a variety of existing garments than to mentally design your own. It was this practice of making samples that customers wanted to buy that eventually encouraged many merchants to begin selling a large variety of finished garments.

Paradoxically, clothes that were made without a particular wearer in mind were able to give the shopper a greater sense of how she chose to define herself and her taste than did custom-made garments, which placed her at the mercy of her dressmaker. Now, shoppers could express their individuality not by specifying their wants but by selecting from a wide variety of garments in many fabrics and styles. But finished dresses and suits and coats took up far more room than had bolts of fabric and cabinets full of buttons. Stores had little choice but to grow to accommodate this new approach to shopping.

The greatest stores remade themselves several times, as shoppers' expectations of comprehensiveness and grandeur increased. Even Stewart's marble palace was soon too small, and it was replaced by the "cast-iron palace" that anchored what became known as "the Ladies' Mile" on lower Fifth Avenue. (It was subsequently acquired as the New York branch of John Wanamaker, which is how the building, which survives, tends to be remembered.)

Nearly all of them followed the Paris model, centered on a vast, open court, with balconies that afforded views of a universe of merchandise. These courts were originally covered in glass, in order to bring light into the interiors of these sprawling buildings. The skylights at Le Bon Marché were engineered by Gustav Eiffel.

After 1900, when electric lighting became reliable, some merchants, including Wanamaker in his ultimate Philadelphia store, decided to forgo the skylights. Still, he kept the spatial grandeur of the court, which he viewed as a kind of civic square, complete with a bronze eagle in the center, which still provides a safe, convenient place for people to meet at the city's heart. The great stores all aspired to be cities in themselves, often incorporating post offices, doctors' clinics, shoe-repair shops, real-estate agencies, banks, and other services. Some department stores even sold automobiles and prefabricated houses. They tried to convince their customers that there was no need to look anywhere else.

*P*aying attention to aspirations: Exclusivity for all

No business whose selling space covered the equivalent of half a dozen or more large city blocks, as all the big-city department stores did, could afford to cater only to the elite customer. They needed to make customers of a large segment of the population.

Especially in the United States, the big stores worked consciously to shape the aspirations of the population at large. By making their stores civic spaces that welcomed almost everyone who was neatly dressed and well-behaved, the stores helped even people who couldn't afford to buy define what material success could be. Nineteenth-century cities were filled with immigrants who came to

America primarily for economic betterment. The stores offered visions of what "making it" looked like. And when these people had "made it," they often became loyal customers.

The department stores also advertised. In nearly every city, daily newspapers and department stores grew large together, mutually dependent upon each other, each regularly adding new sections and new features. John Wanamaker, who is commonly credited with the invention of the full-page newspaper advertisement, said the importance of advertising was not simply to alert people to new products or sales. Rather, it made what was going on at his store part of the news, part of what everyone wanted to know. Advertising made his store part of the consciousness even of people who never dared walk through the door. And the newspapers that were dependent on his advertising were quite willing to tell their readers that the goods available in his store were the newest, best, most stylish and desirable items that could be had. The newspaper helped establish department stores as arenas in which people could, by shopping there, validate their own success.

Department stores were built on a contradiction. They sought to be seen as very high-toned places, even as they appealed to the multitudes. Being thought high-class was desirable, but not if it deterred customers from coming through the door. Moreover, as the stores grew in size, they took on large, relatively low-paid sales forces, including many men and women with little education. The salespeople were required to dress well, but one of the reasons the stores told their clerks to remain silent was to prevent them from speaking in a way that undermined the elite aura the stores sought to project.

Many store managers established codes of service and behavior to ensure that their sales help would remain as discreet as possible. One of the best known and detailed of these was promulgated by Filene's in Boston early in the twentieth century. Clerks were instructed never to ask how much the customer wished to pay, but rather to show the medium-priced item in a particular category and note that other selections were available. They were never to ask a size, but to estimate it, tending to err on the small side. If a customer looked at a particular object, the salesclerk was to describe its merits and never to call an item sweet, cute, or lovely. The clerks were necessary to provide the high level of service that it was believed customers required, but they should never be an obstacle to making a sale. They were to provide personal attention in an impersonal way, leaving the customer free to dream and to buy.

The department store would have been inconceivable without mass industrialization, which produced both a wide range of manufactured goods and the incomes required to purchase them. But most of the great advances in retailing were primarily psychological, designed to make people more comfortable as shoppers and to remove any barriers that would prevent them from buying.

One such was the money-back guarantee, introduced by John Wanamaker in 1865. As he promised in a full-page newspaper advertisement, "Any article that does not fit well, is not of the proper color or quality, does not please the folks at home, or for any reason is not perfectly satisfactory should be brought back to the store at once, and . . . we shall refund the money."

This was a very astute offer in several ways. All shoppers have had the experience of regretting a purchase, and worry that they will do so again. The money-back guarantee meant that the possibility of regret was evaded, a tactic that very likely moved many items, only a small percentage of which were returned. Moreover, the policy made husbands feel less worried about their wives' purchases, because they could exercise a veto. And the gentlemanly tone of the promise, with its implicit affirmation that the store's customers were trustworthy people, flattered the customers and made them feel that they were dealing with a high-class merchant. (Money-back guarantees have largely disappeared during the last half century, probably because shoppers no longer need so much reassurance. But they have recently resurfaced on the Internet, a new retail environment in which shoppers are not entirely certain that they trust the seller, the merchandise, or themselves.)

High-end merchants like Boucicaut and Wanamaker had no monopoly on the psychology and economics of shopping. Perhaps the greatest merchant of all was Frank W. Woolworth, who, between 1879 and 1919, opened more than 1,300 stores in nearly every town in the United States, and others in Canada, Britain, and Germany. His success was based on a strong, simple idea: every item in the store would cost only five cents. Anybody who had a nickel to spend could walk into the store confidently, and that meant that virtually anybody could be a shopper. Woolworth's salesclerks were instructed not to speak to customers until spoken to, or to offer any unsolicited recommendations or judgments on customers' purchases. To shop at Woolworth's was to shop without fear.

This psychological innovation had consequences both for Woolworth's as a business and for its suppliers. In order to provide unusual value to his customers, Woolworth had to create a large chain so that he could order items in bulk and realize savings. Meanwhile, those who wanted to sell to Woolworth's had to work hard to design and make their products inexpensively and reliably. If they could not profitably provide a product that Woolworth could sell for five cents, they knew that they would not sell to the company at all. (Later, Woolworth added ten-cent items, but only very reluctantly.)

Manufacturing to reach a particular price point is universal today, but 120 years ago, it was new and often very difficult. Woolworth understood that only by pressuring manufacturers could he reach the goal he had in mind, which was to make virtually everyone a shopper.

*A*ttending to the contemporary shopper

Woolworth's is extinct in the United States, though chains of dollar stores still operate on Frank Woolworth's original theory. And Woolworth's principle of providing reliable products at the cheapest prices possible is upheld by Wal-Mart and all other mass retailers. It is a logic that has driven the manufacture of retail items to the most impoverished places on earth. But at least in developed countries, even the poor expect to be able to buy. Great retailers like Woolworth and Sam Walton, the founder of Wal-Mart, pay attention to ensure that they are able to do so.

Nowadays, relatively few shoppers are pleased with the quality of the service they get. Surveys of shoppers in a variety of store types rarely indicate that more than half of customers find the quality of service they receive to be satisfactory. Shoppers most frequent complaints are that they can't find a clerk to serve them when they need one, and that the clerks they can find are ignorant of the product line. For many years, manufacturers of small appliances, electronics, cosmetics, and many other kinds of products have followed the dictum that the best information a customer can expect is on the package the product comes in.

It may seem that all the sales help at the stores has disappeared, but that's not true. About 18 percent of the U.S. workforce is in what could be broadly defined as retail sales. This is, however, one of the worst-paid segments of the workforce, and it is one in which the real wages of workers have declined since the mid-1980s. One reason is that this is predominantly a part-time workforce, including a large number of people who are in their first few years of employment, sometimes as young as fourteen. Conventional standards of measuring the productivity of retail workers have risen substantially, partly as the result of falling wages, but mostly because of technologies and business practices that have reduced the skill and knowledge expected of sales help.

The Internet, with its ability to provide large amounts of customized information very quickly, along with its emerging power to simulate understanding, approaches a long-sought ideal of personal service without the danger of personal offense. So far, many more shoppers are using it as an information source, to compensate for the disappearing salesclerk, than as a total shopping environment. In a sense, it is replicating the experience we have with real salespeople. Information is easy to accept. Judgment is more difficult.

That helps explain the delight with which both e-commerce professionals and online shoppers greeted the demise of Boo.com, a much-hyped seller of youthful, fashionable clothes, based in London. In an attempt to make the site "edgy," the text on the site was written with an air of sarcasm and condescension, both toward the goods offered and especially toward those who might want to buy them. Another company has bought the brand and killed the attitude. The lesson is clear. Nobody needs a bitchy interface. Even if we are being served by a computer, we want the right kind of attention.

7
BELONGING

Taste, Lifestyle, and Buying to Fit In

De gustibus non disputandum, advises the ancient proverb— "there's no point in arguing over taste." Taste seems the most personal and subjective of qualities. If you find a morsel of food—or an article of clothing, or a chair—appealing, it seems futile to second-guess your tongue, your nose, your eye, or your convictions.

Proverbs aside, though, people argue about taste all the time. They worry about their own, and question that of others. In its most literal sense, relating to food, taste is not personal but cultural, a shared inclination to like certain flavors, textures, and aromas, while disliking or ignoring others. Growing up appreciating kimchee is part of being Korean, gefilte fish is an element of Eastern-European Jewish heritage, and if you fail to flinch when you find a hairy pig's ear in the scrapple, you're probably from Pennsylvania. All of these preferences have meaning; they announce that you belong to a people and a place, and that those who don't share such tastes don't belong.

When we speak of taste in its broader sense—to describe preferences in clothing, decoration, the arts, or amusement—it likewise cannot be purely personal. If you don't share a taste with others, it is an eccentricity, an aberration, perhaps an antisocial gesture. Taste that is unique to an individual will likely be judged negatively by the group. Even people who celebrate "bad taste" do so in the company of others, and they tend to create standards by which pink plastic flamingos, cheesy science-fiction movies, or vintage polyester clothing are judged bad enough to enjoy.

Taste is not the same as fashion. Fashions come and go, while tastes evolve much more slowly. Most people encounter fashions as phenomena that come from somewhere else, even though they may have helped to create or inspire them. While taste must be shared, it feels like something that comes from within. It is the set of standards we use to filter fashions, so that we can decide whether we might wear a particular piece of clothing, live with a particular pattern in the wallpaper, or enjoy a new song. It is a set of sensibilities that might be shared with a chosen few or with multitudes. Some people's taste induces them to buy into the latest sensations, while other, more conservative sorts seek out items that are variations on a familiar theme. But even the most assiduous novelty-seeker cannot acquire every new gadget, buy every trendy garment, try out every hot hairstyle. All must choose, following their enthusiasms, preferences, dislikes, and values. Thus, everyone has taste.

The concept of taste is based on the idea that objects have meanings, and that people who share the taste can agree on the meaning. In fact, objects have multiple meanings, often contradictory ones. Some people would look at a piece of Brie, and see the soft, creamy cheese as a highly pleasurable indulgence. Others might see it as a mark of snobbishness, or as evidence that the person serving it is striving to gain status (and failing, because the choice is so banal.) President George W. Bush has associated Brie with the sort of people who live on the coasts and have voted against him. Disapproval of what others like is an important component of taste.

While many adolescents try out different kinds of tastes as part of crafting their adult selves, their upbringing and schooling push most young people toward a set of tastes that will evolve, but not change radically, throughout their lives. (And in Internet chat rooms and message boards, young people often identify themselves by the brand of clothing they like best. In certain circles, the moniker "abercrombieguy" says it all.)

Tastes are very important to retailers because long-term customers tend to be the most profitable ones, and shoppers seek out stores that match their tastes. The most influential merchants do not simply introduce fashions; they define and catalyze tastes. They create communities of shared sensibilities and values that can be very enduring. When, for example, The Body Shop cosmetics chain took a stand against elaborate packaging, it set itself apart from all its competitors, and gave young women who were concerned with the environment a way to feel better both physically and morally. The retailer merged objects with values and created a new taste.

Tastes help determine how and where people shop, and how they feel about the goods they see and buy. Nevertheless, the term has an old-fashioned sound to it. At a time when market researchers offer tools that promise to enable retailers to reach ever more precisely defined markets, "taste" seems a vague, unscientific term. Moreover, the word "taste" causes problems because it is most often used to pass judgment on the choices of others. If you say that a woman has good taste, or even just taste, that means you approve of her judgment and probably share her taste. If she has bad taste, you are less likely to seek out her friendship, because you don't see things in the same way. Thus in marketingspeak, the word "taste" has largely been supplanted by neutral terms, such as lifestyle or demographic cluster.

Still, few of us see ourselves as avatars of a lifestyle or members of a cluster. When we shop, we choose some things and reject many others. In doing so, we are exercising our taste.

Reforming taste, creating markets

Taste was a much simpler issue before industrialization vastly increased both the number of objects made and the number of people who were able to afford them. In pre-industrial Europe and

East Asia, taste was determined primarily by small coteries clustered around royal courts and other seats of power. These were the only people who could afford to purchase things, and they were the only people who were judged by their material possessions. When sources of wealth arose that were outside of the control of the ruler or aristocracy, these traditional taste-makers felt threatened. In most cases, though, the newly wealthy sought to obtain exactly the same items in the same styles favored by people in power. Indeed, the inability to distinguish a noble from a rich commoner through his clothes and possessions was precisely what the rulers found objectionable.

With the manufacturing explosion of the nineteenth century, traditional taste-makers were simply overwhelmed by the flood of goods and by a market composed largely of people able to buy for the first time. As often happens when people suddenly acquire the ability to gain possessions, they were drawn to objects that looked "fancy," in the sense that they were highly ornamented or extremely showy. They lacked the background and experience that would enable them to make subtle distinctions among items. Understandably, they often chose the biggest, boldest things they could afford.

Moreover, most manufacturers had no links to craft traditions, or to the design principles that emerged from them. They discovered quickly that it was as easy to produce ornate or elaborate designs as simpler ones. Indeed, sometimes it was cheaper to do so, because a busy design can disguise poorly joined seams and other imperfections. The items were purchased by inexperienced buyers who equated luxuriant decoration with high-class living. Exuberant ornament appeared both on items that are traditionally decorative, such as furniture, and on utilitarian items, such as stoves.

Dense decoration was so characteristic of the nineteenth century that it virtually defines what we call Victorian. Nevertheless, throughout the nineteenth century there were numerous efforts—especially in England, the first cluttered country, and later in Europe and North America—to reform taste by simplifying ornament, reconnecting it with tradition and making it more "rational." These taste reformers operated from an elite perspective, though the means they used, such as public education in the arts, museums and exhibitions, and publicizing products they admired, sought to engage a large buying public. To contemporary eyes, the products of reform often appear as ornate as the items the reformers reviled. Nevertheless, efforts to improve the tastes of manufacturers and those who bought their wares have had lasting impact.

Perhaps the most important aesthetic reform effort came from a traditional source of taste, the monarchy. Prince Albert, Queen Victoria's consort, chose to continue the ancient tradition of royal taste-making in a distinctly nineteenth-century way. He argued that British manufacturers were in danger of losing markets to foreign competitors who offered goods that were better looking and better made. He believed the solution to this commercial challenge was not to harangue manufacturers but to educate them, along with the public, in matters of aesthetics and design.

The Great Exhibition of 1851, held in the Crystal Palace in Hyde Park, had precedents in the great medieval fairs, but it was also as modern as a department store. It exposed a wide public to a world of material possibilities. By educating the public about art and industry, Prince Albert and its other organizers hoped to improve both.

An important legacy of the exhibition was the creation of a group of public museums, one of which, the South Kensington Museum, later renamed the Victoria and Albert Museum, was highly influential, especially in the United States. Most other great museums were treasure houses, often located in former royal palaces and consisting of former royal collections. The Victoria and Albert Museum was conceived from the start as an educational institution, whose aim was both aesthetic and economic improvement. Its message was that art was not for the glory of God, as it had been in churches, or for the glory of the king, as it was in palaces. Art was now for the consumer. And one's choice of material goods was not simply a symptom of economic improvement. Shopping could be an instrument of cultural improvement as well. By becoming more conscious of your taste, you could belong to a better class of people.

America, which lacked both aristocracy and artistic masterpieces, was inspired by both London's exhibition and its new museum. The great Centennial Exhibition of 1876 introduced Americans both to the telephone and to Japanese art. One of its buildings became the home of a new museum (later the Philadelphia Museum of Art) whose associated school placed particular emphasis on the application of the arts to manufacturing. Many of the Centennial's industrial exhibits were purchased and displayed for decades by the Smithsonian Institution, which grew into a larger American version of the London museum complex initiated by Prince Albert. Many other institutions, such as the Brooklyn Museum and the Art Institute of Chicago, followed the Victoria and Albert's model directly, and though most American museums have acquired their share of treasures, they continue today to present themselves as educational institutions. A few, notably New York's Museum of Modern Art, have regarded themselves as molders of public taste.

It was not a coincidence that the museum and the department store arose at the same time, and that their activities have often overlapped. (Department stores have frequently shown important exhibitions of art and design, a practice that has largely ended in the United States, but continues in Europe and especially Japan.) Both encourage sensuous browsing. Those who visit them are open to new ways of seeing. Both are foundries of taste.

Turning the avant-garde into customers: The genius of Liberty

In addition to the mainstream, commercially oriented design reform proposed by Prince Albert, two other taste-changing movements emerged in England during the nineteenth century, which helped change the way people shopped. They did so, in large part, because of the influence of an artistically savvy entrepreneur, Arthur Lazenby Liberty. He understood that a consumer society produces many tastes. He appealed to the tastes not of the mainstream, but rather of smaller groups of dissenting materialists who cared very much about the objects in their lives. He offered the goods that embodied their principles, and his store became a gathering place where people with strong, minority tastes could feel that they belonged.

Through its atmosphere and offerings, every successful store creates its own clientele. Liberty went farther and helped define a whole alternative culture. He did so by recognizing that many people shopped to realize their values, and that even those opposed to prevailing standards of dress and decoration could constitute a valuable market. Liberty's customers may have been trying to show their superiority to those with a more quantitative and conventional view of luxury. But they consumed just as conspicuously, and even more profitably for the merchant who found a way to sell them the styles they wanted.

The first of the avant-garde groups whose members Liberty cultivated was the aesthetic movement, which celebrated the ideal of beauty uncompromised by any moral obligation, or by any need to reflect the spirit of a time or culture. "Beauty is the wonder of wonders," wrote Oscar Wilde, the movement's poster boy, in *The Picture of Dorian Gray.* "It is only shallow people who do not judge by appearances."

Aestheticism was an outgrowth of romanticism, and its adherents professed belief in Keats's dictum, "A thing of beauty is a joy forever." Adherents of aestheticism professed that beauty transcends fashion, though they devoted much of their energy to fighting the fashions of the time and proposing alternatives of their own. Wilde, for one, understood that the pursuit of perfection, which characterized aestheticism, would inevitably lead to dissatisfaction and ever-increasing consumption. "A cigarette is the perfect type of a perfect pleasure," he wrote in *Dorian Gray,* a novel whose subject was the pursuit of the perfect and the corruption it engendered. "It is exquisite, and it leaves one unsatisfied."

Because they believed strongly that beauty could be found in all cultures, aesthetes were always on the lookout for exotic styles. For example, Japanese furniture and woodcuts, shown at the London exhibition of 1862, had an impact that lasted for decades.

In 1875, when Liberty opened a shop of his own on Regent Street, it was called East India House, and it specialized in imported silks in colorful prints, which quickly became part of the aesthetic look. Soon afterward, Liberty hired English designers to create similar prints that became equally fashionable. Beauty might be eternal, but there was always new beauty to discover. Even among people who thought themselves beyond fashion, there would still be those who wanted to be the first to display the newest discovery. Three decades later, Liberty was continuing to market new kinds of exoticism, including a homegrown variety adapted from ancient Celtic objects.

In 1884, Liberty decided to open a dress department and hired the architect, designer, writer, and critic E. W. Godwin to manage it. This was an inspiration. Godwin was one of the most imposing artistic and intellectual figures of his age, and a well-known advocate for simpler, more comfortable and attractive ways of dressing. (Prada, the Italian fashion retailer pulled off a similar coup recently by hiring the Dutch architect Rem Koolhaas as artistic consultant. Koolhaas may not be the world's best known architect, but he has tremendous cachet as a thinker and designer, and Prada purchasers will likely have heard of him. He is also a consultant to Condé Nast, the publisher of *Vogue, Lucky,* and other shopping-oriented magazines.)

Liberty had another reason for recruiting Godwin: He was widely known to be the lover of Ellen Terry, celebrated at the time as the greatest actress of the London stage. She wore the dresses that Liberty was selling, and so did many other women who were, as the *Grove Dictionary of Art* ingenuously puts it, "rebelling against the tyranny of fashion." By emulating people like Terry and Wilde, these buyers subscribed to a new kind of oppression, the tyranny of celebrity. (Today, some celebrities are tastes in themselves: Powerhouses like Oprah Winfrey, Martha Stewart, and Michael Jordan are potent endorsers of products, in large part, because they offer models to which buyers can aspire.)

Some shopped at Liberty because the store's merchandise embodied their ideas; others wanted to dress like a star. But all could feel that they belonged.

The other avant-garde coterie Liberty cultivated was the arts-and-crafts movement. Unlike the aesthetes, the arts-and-crafts adherents attributed the ugliness of industrial production not to the vulgar sensibilities of buyers, but rather to the methods of production itself. The writer and designer William Morris, later to be known for his floral prints and adjustable chair, argued that both objects and human lives had been impoverished by the disappearance of craft. Those who make a thing from beginning to end give it a unique quality that cannot be achieved when many people produce the object by performing small repetitive tasks. Karl Marx would later echo this argument, concentrating on the plight of the worker alienated from his labor. Morris believed the salvation of the worker lay in the revival and adaptation of pre-industrial means of production.

It seems amazing that a movement that grew from a handful of nineteenth-century intellectuals with medieval pretensions became an international phenomenon that lasted three quarters of a century. Nevertheless, the privileged desire for a more caring, less wasteful, more humane kind of materialism is still a strong force at the turn of the twenty-first century. And now, as then, it sells quite a lot of products.

Liberty took a pragmatic approach to the arts-and-crafts movement. While the aesthetic movement produced recognizable and important architecture and design, particularly the furniture of Charles Locke Eastlake, Liberty was most interested in its fabric, clothing, and other soft goods. By contrast, the arts-and-crafts movement's greatest strength was in furniture design, metalwork, and other components of the home. Indeed, the products of the two movements were compatible because although arts-and-crafts philosophy had a moral component that aesthetes rejected, there was a considerable overlap between their buildings, furnishings, clothing, and objects.

For the most part, Liberty ignored the principles of arts-and-crafts. He hired excellent designers and craftsmen to produce prototypes to be sold in his store, but he often modified the designs to be produced in factories. Essentially, he reduced what had been a movement to merely a look. And in so doing, he drew a lot of buyers who were young, who had aesthetic and intellectual aspirations, and who wished to make a statement through what they bought.

In fairness to Liberty, the manufacturing methods advocated by the arts-and-crafts movement could produce only small numbers of very expensive objects. Yet most of those attracted to the arts-and-crafts movement were not the wealthiest people but, rather, educated children of an upper middle class that had been made possible by industrialization. Many products based on arts-and-crafts designs were produced in the late nineteenth and early twentieth century—in Britain, Germany, the United States, Scandinavia, and elsewhere—but few were made according to arts-and-crafts principles.

Liberty's achievement was that he helped to create a new kind of shopper, a shopper who wanted gowns that would flow, not flounce, who preferred inexpensive colorful stones to the expensive glitter of diamonds, who saw integrity in oak and only an oppressive darkness in mahogany. At the turn of the century, he would play a major role in popularizing the sensuous, tendril-like forms of the international movement known as art nouveau. This time, the new style was, at least in Britain, unrelated to any intellectual movement. It was pure novelty and pure pleasure.

American taste reform: Forging diffuse communities

The United States is so large and diffuse that it could probably never produce a single store as influential as Liberty's. But many Americans were powerfully drawn to the integrity and simplicity that the arts-and-crafts movement promised. They wanted to buy it themselves, and perhaps even build it themselves. Rather than build stores, arts-and-crafts entrepreneurs started publications that engendered, even among those distant from any fellow believers, a sense of belonging to an important movement. And they built mailing lists of like-minded people, which were precursors to the niche marketing and virtual communities that are so important a part of contemporary shopping.

In 1900, Gustav Stickley opened his furniture factory, to produce large quantities of arts-and-crafts or "mission-style" furniture for a middle-class market. The following year, he began his magazine, *The Craftsman,* and in 1904, he began selling plans for craftsman-style bungalows his readers could build for themselves. An estimated $10 million worth of such houses were built by 1915.

The furniture and decorative items Stickley sold embodied a simplicity and integrity their buyers didn't feel they could find in the goods available elsewhere. But those who bought these items weren't rebelling against the idea of buying things. They were simply buying things they liked better, and they expected their maker to make a profit. As Elbert Hubbard, another art-and-crafts entrepreneur, said, "The World of Commerce is just as honorable as the World of Art, and a trifle more necessary."

Hubbard, who is best known for his association with the Roycrofters, an arts-and-crafts community in East Aurora, New York, also served for a time as an executive of the Larkin Manufacturing Co. of Buffalo, an early and ambitious American attempt to identify alternative markets. Larkin, which had begun as a seller of soap by mail, first offered decorative items as premiums to encourage sale of the soap, and gradually moved into selling a variety of items to those on their mailing list. Aside from the soap, nearly everything that Larkin offered appealed to people with an arts-and-crafts sensibility, and Larkin products gained a reputation for being very well made. Thus, while Sears Roebuck and Montgomery Ward were using their huge catalogues to appeal to a vast but unfocused market, Larkin sought what would now be called a niche market. Larkin is remembered today for having commissioned Frank Lloyd Wright to design its headquarters building, which, though it was demolished half a century ago, is one of the most celebrated office buildings ever constructed. What is less widely known is that almost the entire building was given over to what would now be called a database. It was a filing system, containing cards that recorded every purchase by each of the firm's customers, and which was used to determine which customers would be offered which of the company's items. Thus, while the entire product line appealed to a distinct segment of American taste, Larkin management also knew about the particular enthusiasms and buying habits of each customer. The company was able to use this information to design new products, and offer them to the customers who were most likely to buy.

The Larkin management's ideas were far in advance of the technology available to execute them. Today, the entire contents of this building, and the work of its hundreds of file keepers, could be handled by a few people at personal computers. And the Internet seems destined to become the way in which people anywhere can find others who share their tastes, and vendors to supply the products that embody these tastes.

The Larkin experiment was distinctly American in that it tried to create a community of consumers who were in widely separated locations. Like the Internet, it sought to substitute information for proximity. The success the company enjoyed, at least temporarily, testified to the commercial potential of those who had reservations about the goods that were commonly sold and were willing to seek out an alternative.

American arts-and-crafts furniture went out of style for more than fifty years, before its rediscovery during the 1970s and the ensuing sharp rise in prices. Arts-and-crafts ideas endure in unlikely ways. The domestic exertions of Martha Stewart reflect arts-and-crafts principles in their emphasis on being laboriously handmade. Stewart runs a business empire that is based on the aspiration to actually make something, even something as ephemeral as a Thanksgiving table setting, with real care.

And at the turn of the twenty-first century, an industry has arisen to cater to the desire for simplicity. It consists of people who want to organize your closet and reorganize your mind. In particular, it consists of people who want to sell you the fewer but truly pleasurable and authentic things that make life truly worthwhile. *Real Simple,* a magazine published by the Time Inc. division of AOL–Time Warner, serves this growing market. But its articles and its advertising give a good picture of what simplicity means in our time. In one recent issue, the advertisements suggest that simplicity might mean a really peaceful cup of creamy coffee, with nobody bothering you, or youthful skin, achieved through natural means and cutting-edge technology. Simplicity might even mean a sport-utility vehicle, not a gas-guzzling truck overloaded with gadgets, but rather a vehicle that could carry you to personal communion with the beauty and majesty of nature.

The most revealing *Real Simple* article was about the pleasures of taking a nice, hot bath. The necessities for achieving "pure pleasure" in your own home included a chrome towel-warmer, a plush mat, a terry tub-pillow, a storage cabinet, a lamp that casts a gentle glow, a plywood tray that holds sea sponges, a sisal exfoliating cloth, and a dark-bristled Acca Kappa brush. By the third page of the article, we've already spent more than $1,000, and we haven't even reached the teas, the oils, the salts, or the milks, nor have we purchased a single towel.

In a letter, a reader provides the rationale. "Keeping it simple does not mean reducing the quality of one's lifestyle; it means putting first things first. It's fine not to feel guilt over guilty pleasures while keeping your life focused, pleasurable and worthwhile."

While not everyone defines simplicity so hedonistically, the simplicity movement is one symptom of a malaise that permeates our shopping-saturated world. In a department store, or even a supermarket, most shoppers are confronted with thousands of items that not only fail to meet their immediate needs, but which arouse active distaste or disapproval. Some who most strongly resist shopping tell researchers that they are made physically ill by the overabundance of wasteful and ugly products and the spectacle of large crowds eager to possess them. Even those who like to shop sometimes feel moments of disgust with sheer profusion of stuff and with their own acquisitive impulses. While the logical response to such revulsion should simply be not to shop, more often than not it results in a decision to buy something that will reflect your own taste and superiority.

The message for marketers is that this so-called new consumer, this searcher for authenticity and real pleasure, is willing to spend more, and thus promises a higher profit margin. New consumers need to be flattered for their superior values and discriminating tastes. They must feel that they belong to a more virtuous group of consumers who understand how to live better lives. New consumers are rebelling against the incessant commercialism of the time much as the arts-and-crafts movement reacted to the proliferation of cheap, ugly goods during the nineteenth century: by trying to buy better. The desire the arts-and-crafts movement first articulated and which the new consumer echoes—to return to an authentic, premodern integrity—is a constant in American culture. We want simultaneously to do the right thing, feel the real thing, and have everything.

Explaining consumer behavior—Veblen and emulation

At the turn of the twentieth century, when Liberty & Co. was enjoying its greatest influence and arts-and-crafts-based businesses were burgeoning in the United States, the American economist and social thinker Thorstein Veblen published *The Theory of the Leisure Class*. It is the most lastingly influential, or at least unavoidable, critique of acquisition and display ever written. Even if one disagrees with Veblen, it is difficult to avoid using terms he coined, such as "conspicuous consumption."

Essentially, Veblen argued that at least from the time humanity passed from "savagery" into "barbarism," powerful people have expressed their power by being able to avoid participating in the processes of manufacture. Because such leisure is often invisible, such people began to seek out valuable items as marks of their higher status, thus setting off a never-ending competition. "In any community where goods are held in severalty," he wrote, "it is necessary, in order to his own peace of mind, that an individual should possess as large a portion of goods as others with whom he is accustomed to class himself; and it is extremely gratifying to possess something more than others." Buying, in Veblen's view, seems to be about belonging to a group, but it inevitably turns competitive, as each person seeks to modestly outdo those with whom he compares himself. For Veblen, emulation is the key mechanism by which this vicious consumption cycle is driven. One looks to the people at the top or, more likely, to those who slightly outrank you, and seeks to have the same things they do, and something more besides. Your taste in goods is thus determined entirely by people with power and wealth.

Veblen shared with members of the arts-and-crafts movement a disgust for the excess and waste that was being produced by mass manufacturing. Unlike them, he saw pre-industrial cultures to be driven by the same urges. If they were less wasteful, it was only because they lacked the technology to consume so intensely. Veblen was skeptical of the arts-and-crafts movement because he said, correctly, it was not changing the relationships within the society. It was simply another form of conspicuous waste, just another of what he termed "pecuniary canons of taste." The alternative markets that Liberty, Stickley, or Larkin served could be seen, in Veblen's terms, as particularly privileged segments of the leisure class, one that applied a great deal of time to studying beauty, style, and other not immediately productive subjects. Its members bought things to embody their greater personal power and sensitivity.

A bit more than a century after Veblen's book was published, only a small part of the population in developed countries is directly engaged in manufacturing. Moreover, most industrial workers, at least in Europe and North America, work shorter hours than many managers and professionals, and they have substantial buying power as well. Our society is thus composed almost entirely of the leisure class, as Veblen described it, although most of us may not feel ourselves to have much leisure. We are engaged in a mania of consumption just as intense as Veblen predicted. More and more people own houses that are larger and larger, and ever more crowded with stuff.

But the mechanisms of taste creation and emulation are infinitely more complicated than Veblen imagined. His theory actually allowed for people to choose the consumption groups to which they wished to belong, but he generally assumed that there was but a single ladder of status advancement. Today, we don't merely have a variety of ladders, but rather a multidimensional matrix of taste and status, on which we can climb in many directions, and in which "high" and "low" culture intersect in unexpected ways. One can never be entirely sure of one's own absolute superiority or another's "pecuniary strength." The high-consumption society gives us much subtler choices about how to spend our time and present ourselves to others than Veblen ever imagined.

One wonders what Veblen would have made of hip-hop culture. In their insistent demands for respect and their flaunting of expensive, traditionally high-status items, many gangsta rappers seem to have stepped right out of *The Theory of the Leisure Class*. They present themselves as transgressive figures, people who got their money from drug-dealing, pimping, robbery, and other kinds of criminal activity, yet their pride resides in being able to outspend the establishment, buying exactly the same goods. In what they choose to purchase, they emulate those they claim to revile. Coming from outside of establishment culture, their message is that they can overpower the powerful, even on the establishment's own terms. But they don't pretend that they do not enjoy the material rewards. The situation becomes even more complicated when you consider that hip-hop began as an expression of ghetto style, but that it thrives financially because it is embraced by a mostly white audience of suburban youths. The luxury cars and wristwatches that rappers celebrate are very likely as attractive to the young fans' parents as they are to the rappers. Is contemporary hip-hop, then, merely a scary mask that some adolescents don to convince themselves and others that they aren't merely clones of their acquisitive parents, or is it a real rebellion?

If you are a critic of consumption and a follower of Veblen, you may conclude that hip-hop is simply emulation in a new guise. But if you are trying to sell products, you will more likely see hip-hop as distinctive and significant. Guises are important. Who people imagine themselves to be is just as important as who they are. The same is true of goods. Because hip-hop has assimilated a lot of former preppy styles, the same shirt can represent either ghetto status or Ivy League aspirations. If you are trying to market the shirt, however, you must understand the distinction and tailor your messages accordingly.

For the first half of the twentieth century, some retailers understood the concept of creating a community of taste to inspire shopper loyalty. In many European cities, such as Munich, Vienna, Paris, Glasgow, and Barcelona, some shop-owners cultivated artists and designers, creating a community of patrons for their designs. Most large retailers and nearly all manufacturers, however, aimed at a large market and assumed that there was but a single ladder of taste that their customers aspired to ascend. Department stores featured departments called "better dresses," usually on higher floors, for shoppers who wanted to move up.

The 1924 declaration by General Motors chief executive Alfred Sloan that the company's aim was to produce "a car for every purse and purpose," demonstrated a belief in Veblen's concept of emulation. At the top of the line was Cadillac, below that were Buick, Oldsmobile, LaSalle, and Pontiac. The least prestigious, most popular car, the Chevrolet, was sometimes called "a baby Cadillac," a nickname that recognized that all of these cars represented a single continuum of values. There were, to be sure, slightly different meanings ascribed to each make of car, but it was understood that nearly everyone aspired to a Cadillac.

Americans were pioneers in introducing psychological principles into marketing, packaging, and advertising during the early twentieth century. The traditional approach had been to cite the characteristics and advantages of the product, but once psychologists became involved, packaging and advertising were used to give the product meaning. Walter Dill Scott, a pioneer in psychological advertising, expressed this concept in 1917: "The actual effect of modern advertising is not so much to convince as to suggest." Such suggestions could go far beyond the meaning of the product. With the Model T, for example, Henry Ford had produced an economical and practical automobile. But Sloan's General Motors product line was more than a bunch of cars. It was a widely understood measure of personal achievement and status.

Before World War II, use of psychology to sell things was based largely on conjecture. Immediately after, marketing consultants began doing depth interviews, administering tests, and creating other tools to try to probe people's deepest feelings about consumer goods. Partly as a result, more products deliberately embodied contradictions. Tide, the first heavy-duty artificial laundry detergent, sought out to be perceived as powerful, yet mild, and it did so by carefully balancing the yellow and dark-blue design of its packaging. Such tricks were chronicled in Vance Packard's 1955 best-seller *The Hidden Persuaders,* an account of consumer manipulation that many people found alarming.

Still, despite more diligent research, marketing psychologists assumed that reactions to products were universal and that everyone would find the same meanings in them. Those who dissented from mainstream tastes were not worth thinking about. There were, for example, car-buyers who did not subscribe to General Motors' ladder of progress and instead purchased Volkswagens, a revolt that was largely ignored. One Ford executive dismissed the importance of this group, calling them "gray-flannel nonconformists." Unlike Arthur Liberty, he did not recognize such materialist dissenters as a potentially profitable clientele. Ford wasn't organized to respond to minority tastes, and as a result, it lost market share to foreign competitors who were.

There is plenty of evidence that post–World War II shoppers did feel they belonged to a unified society. Income differences were diminishing, and powerful mass media, especially network television, were providing everyone with the same frames of reference. Because manufacturers and large retailers used television and mass magazines to reach their customers, they had little choice but to suppress differences in taste and desires, and try to establish a common meaning for their products. And for a while it worked.

*L*ifestyles, clusters, and markets of one: Classifying today's shopper

The post–World War II age of the mass market began to give way to today's hyperdifferentiation of the shopper during the 1960s. It became clear during that decade that there were limits to togetherness. Not everyone bought into the same values. Not everyone subscribed to the same consensus. Marketers had long been fascinated with psychoanalysis, which seemed to offer universally applicable insights for understanding and manipulating a mass market. Now, they switched their attention to sociology, which documented differences among and promised clues for reaching an increasingly diverse consuming public. No longer did it make sense to speak of one American way of life. Now, everyone had a lifestyle.

During the 1960s and 1970s, polling helped politicians define their constituencies, and manufacturers find their markets. Rather than merely find out what potential customers thought about a specific product, new social-research techniques studied the customers themselves. By probing their backgrounds, their beliefs, their habits, and their goals, they sought to understand shopping as part of an overall pattern of behavior, and thus to understand how products fit into their lives.

This changing view of the shopper coincided with, and very likely accelerated changes in communications and information systems. General interest magazines gave way to niche publications whose editorial content was conceived to support advertising catering to a narrow but well-defined market. Videocassette recorders and cable and satellite television decreased the pervasive hold of network television. Scanner systems in supermarkets made it possible to determine the buying habits of individual families, and credit card data could be mined for information on buying habits.

In 1978, SRI, a contract research company that is an offshoot of Stanford University, introduced VALS (values and life styles). This model fused psychology, sociology, and demographic data into a typology of consumer behavior. It broke the market into nine categories, with "survivors"—people who have no money to spend—on the bottom, and the "integrated"—people who have reached the consumer nirvana of having enough to spend and a firm, sane notion of how to spend it—at the top. The most interesting and profitable people were in the middle. "Emulators," consumers who followed Veblen's "outer-directed" pattern of comparing themselves to those just above them on the status ladder, were estimated to constitute a bit less than twenty percent of the consumer market. Other, "inner-directed," categories of people who sought experience rather than goods, or who viewed their purchasing within a framework of social consciousness were estimated to be just about as numerous. Countless companies began to use VALS, and in 1983, Arnold Mitchell, the developer of the model, wrote an influential book called *The Nine American Lifestyles*. Despite the growing reliance of companies on VALS, it was largely a theoretical construct, unsupported by actual survey results. Only when it was refined and reintroduced as VALS2, in 1989, was the model backed by solid numbers.

During the 1980s, the ability of computers to collate and compare data gave rise to demographic clustering, which purports to break the population into categories that are more or less self-defining. Nowadays, marketers vie with one another to coin snappy terms for ever more narrowly defined consumer groups. Thus, supermarket owners are counseled that their profits depend on finding the right mix to respond to their customers' different attitudes toward fitness. Are they, as one model proposes, "physical fantastics," who keep fit for their health, "active attractives," who keep fit to enhance their appearance, "hard-living hedonists," or "noninterested nihilists"? This methodology yields dozens of glibly named categories. Michael Weiss's 2000 book *The Clustered World* depicts an America broken into sixty-two clusters, with names like "Winner's Circle," "Pools and Patios," "Pickups and Shotguns," "Hispanic Mix," "Scrub Pine Flats," "New Empty Nesters," and "Gray Collar." The largest such cluster, "Kids and Cul-de-sacs," comprises only 3.5 percent of the population.

Even these distinctive labels are applied to geographical areas as large as a zip code district or a census tract. Yet on a single block, you can find one house filled with South Asian sculpture, another that resembles an Ivy League common room, and yet another that's decorated in a rain-forest motif, wallpapered with oversized palm fronds and overgrown with luxuriant tropical plants. The neighbors may vote alike, and live in houses that are structurally similar, but the way in which they spend money to define their environments, and themselves, could hardly be more different. These differences are exactly what those who want to sell us products want to identify and respond to.

That's where the Internet comes in, with software "cookies" that track our surfing and programs like the one mentioned in chapter six that can discern shared patterns of consumption that need not make any sense whatsoever. This technology assumes that we do belong to communities of people who share our tastes and desires, but we have no idea of who these people are. We are alone with our passions to acquire, and as for who our soulmates are, only the computer knows for sure.

The ultimate consequence of such knowledge is the "market of one," in which sellers will know so much about each potential buyer that they will be able to custom-design both the products they offer and the sales pitch individually. This is a seductive idea, though it may well prove to be a pipe dream. What we buy is more about the values we share with at least a few others. It is not really about those qualities that define us as individuals.

In fact, micromarketing is very much about fine-tuning the selling message—and very little about tailoring the product—to the tastes and wishes of the individual or even of the demographic cluster.

For example, a business article on Natuzzi, an Italian manufacturer of leather-upholstered furniture, noted that thirteen different stores at Pennsylvania's King of Prussia Mall sell the company's products. This seems to fly in the face of the belief in specialized markets. A visit to the mall showed that what the stores offered was overwhelmingly similar, though the meanings the stores ascribed to the sofas and chairs differ.

At JC Penney, that most middle-American retail chain, the pieces on display were bulky, with great dewlaps hanging from their back and arms, as if designed to fill a sprawling suburban home. At Bloomingdale's, by contrast, the furniture was less overweight, more tailored, designed for urban environments where floor space is at a premium, and where ostentatious comfort is less desirable.

Elsewhere, the differences in the furniture were smaller, while the differences in its meaning were more insistent. For example, Domain, a furniture store, evokes an atmosphere of exotic disarray, with fringed lamps, old carpets, and every seating piece covered with decorative pillows and colorful fabrics. (You have to buy a whole lot of stuff to get a look like this.) Among its offerings are a huge, overstuffed chair and ottoman called "Havana." This is pre-Castro Cuba, though really it's more Hollywood. (One can imagine Sidney Greenstreet taking it easy in the "Havana.") Meanwhile, at Restoration Hardware, one finds the "Buster," a similarly overstuffed chair, that because of its design and the retail environment in which it is sold conveys a very different message. "Buster" is so puffed up and outsized that it borders on the ridiculous. Like a big, friendly dog, the chair makes you smile. Smart people have labored to make it effectively dumb. It evokes pop art and Betty Boop, but like so many items in this store, it also speaks of a vaguely remembered grandparents' time, when things were more real and experience more naïve and heartfelt. Irony and nostalgia may seem to be conflicting attitudes, but an easy chair can embody both at once.

Just as Liberty & Co. did, Domain and Restoration Hardware sell sensibility. The difference is that Liberty created his community of tasteful shoppers with a very distinctive set of products, which satisfied both his customers' ideals and their desires. In our fragmented world of demographic clusters and micromarkets, we're all buying more or less the same chair. But we're doing so for sixty-two different reasons.

8
CELEBRATION

Spending Christmas with Family

$\mathcal{T}$o celebrate Christmas you have to shop, whether you like to or not. Even those who say they like to shop tell market researchers that holiday crowds, traffic, and time pressures often make them tense, weary, and distraught. Many shoppers like the decorations and the Christmas music, but they also complain that these nice things appear too early. Two full months of "Jingle Bells" jangle the nerves, yet there never seems to be enough time to do all that needs to be done.

It may seem that shopping should be inessential to the celebration of a holiday that celebrates a miraculous event. But during the last two centuries, Christmas has evolved into a celebration of family and of caring, and presents seem to be the way in which we reaffirm our ties to family and friends. Shopping is at the center of this holiday because it is a show of love, which is why buying for Christmas is so emotionally taxing.

There's no question that holiday shopping is important to the economy. In the United States, about one-third of all retail spending takes place in the holiday shopping season that begins in mid-November and ends in mid-January. Depending on who's counting, average spending on the holidays in the United States runs $850 to

$1,150 per household. In early 2001, after a Christmas in which sales grew, but not as dramatically as in previous years, several states announced possible budget shortfalls. Sales tax revenues hadn't increased as much as was expected, so some state services were in peril. And during the following Christmas season, after the September 11 attacks, shoppers were encouraged to think of their purchases as a blow against terrorists. You might not consider that if you cut back your Christmas shopping, the local schools might not be able to afford new textbooks—or the world economy might be jeopardized; but that's how the system works.

Indeed, people's awareness of the economic importance of Christmas contributes to the guilt many feel about their observance of the holiday. Every year, people complain that Christmas has been overwhelmed by materialism, and that its true meaning is lost as we waste our time and our wealth buying things for one another that nobody needs.

Yet the power of Christmas—spiritual and emotional, as well as economic—has been on the increase in recent decades. Christmas represents continuity and kinship, even as families have become dispersed geographically, and have taken on configurations that would have seemed shocking or wildly unconventional half a century ago. In the absence of rules or widely shared expectations about what constitutes a family or how it should behave, families are increasingly defined by their members. But such relationships require some outward sign, some concrete acknowledgment that the ties exist.

Christmas can sometimes seem a great shakedown, in which you are coerced into buying presents for people you don't really know. The clerk's perennial question "How much do you want to spend?" forces the Christmas shopper into assigning an economic value to every relationship. And it can be very embarrassing if the person for whom you have bought a gift turns out to have spent either much more or much less on you.

Still, the evolved Christmas shopper can also forget worrying about the imbalances endemic to gift-giving and use the opportunity to engage with other people. Having to buy gifts reminds you how old your nieces are, and forces you to know something about what girls their age like nowadays and to decide whether you're willing to buy it for them. It makes you think about people to whom you were once close and with whom you want to maintain a connection. It forces you to think about your parents or children living far away, and about what you can do to improve their lives. In the context of life-long relationships, Christmas presents seem insignificant. But they keep people thinking about one another, and they provide a concrete affirmation that we are doing so. We all go our own ways, then hope that the things we buy in the stores in December and wrap in red and green paper will be enough to hold us together.

People need celebrations. They give texture to life and mark moments in time. All holidays have, at least at their inception, something of the holy about them, but they also offer a release from responsibility that often leads to eating, drinking, and spending. As we have seen, medieval fairs were usually held on feast days, both because people felt free on those days, and because there is always something serious about spending your wealth.

From a theological perspective, Easter, not Christmas, is the chief Christian holiday, because it commemorates the resurrection of Jesus, a cosmic event. Christmas, by contrast, is more of a domestic event. It's easy for people to identify with the joyous birth of a child. Still, it seems clear that the shopping-and-Santa side of Christmas has enhanced the holiday's importance for religious Christians, much as the incorporation of Hanukkah as part of the year-end festival has increased observance of that holiday by religious Jews.

Today, most of us seem to deal with the holiday's dual nature mostly by deploring it, even as we indulge. Some people, though, find ingenious ways of maintaining their moral rectitude. One woman called into an NPR program to say that her family had moved the exchange of gifts to January 6, the feast of the Epiphany, or Three Kings, when the Magi presented their gifts to Jesus. They did so, she explained, in order to be true to the original gospel narrative—and so that they could take advantage of the postholiday markdowns. Thus the caller was able to feel righteous even as she got a better bargain. We like to feel that we are participating in the deeper meaning of the holiday. But we like the presents, too. And who can pass up a sale?

The deep roots of indulgence

"The impulse to spend seizes everyone. He who the whole year has taken pleasure in saving . . . becomes suddenly extravagant. People are not only more generous towards themselves, but also towards their fellow-men. A stream of presents pours itself out on all sides."

The writer is Libanius, a philosopher of rhetoric in fourth-century Constantinople, describing the celebration throughout the Roman Empire of the Calends holiday, which occurred about January 1. It was one of a group of observances that, in Roman lands, constituted a holiday season around the time of the winter solstice. There was also Saturnalia, celebrated on December 17, with cross-dressing and role reversal between slaves and masters, and the celebration of the Invincible Sun, on December 25, the chief observance of a very powerful cult that originated in Syria in the later Roman Empire.

Most people celebrated two or more of these pre-Christian winter holidays, creating a holiday season that parallels what we have today. The season began with end-of-harvest festivals, of which Americans' Thanksgiving Day is a contemporary analogue. The biggest holidays, however, came somewhat later, near the winter solstice, when supplies of fresh foods were dwindling. After the holidays, people would have to get by on provisions that had been smoked, cured, dried, pickled, or very carefully stored. (Sauerkraut on New Year's Day, a tradition in parts of America where Germans settled, recalls this fact.) The holiday season was not so much a religious observance or a harvest festival as it was a final splurge before the coming of lean times.

There is something defiant about holding the most lavish of holidays in the face of the most dangerous months of the year, even though much of the food would have rotted had it not been eaten. It is important that the biggest of such holidays came at or after the solstice, when the promise of longer days offered reassurance that spring would come. Still, expending so many resources at the coldest and most difficult time of year is frightening. A holiday provides a social and spiritual occasion to do so.

Around the time Libanius was writing, a new holiday was emerging among Christians to celebrate the birth of their prophet and savior. It became fixed on December 25. Because nobody knew the actual date of Christ's birth, the leaders of the early Christian church were clearly trying to redirect to Christian purposes the energies already expended on the verge-of-winter holiday season that had existed for centuries.

In many ways, though, the pagan nature of this festival has never really gone away. Our celebrations of Thanksgiving, Hanukkah, Christmas, Kwanzaa, New Year's, and Three Kings often seem to be contemporary expressions of very ancient holiday traditions, whose details shift from day to day, but fundamental expressions remain the same. For example, Americans once exchanged presents on New Year's, not Christmas. And the celebration of New Year's Eve, with its whistles, funny hats, and drunkenness keeps at least a hint of the old Saturnalian misrule.

The early Christian leaders were concerned that old pagan spirit might overwhelm the religious significance of Christmas, so they created Advent, the four weeks leading up to Christmas intended as a period of fasting, prayer, and reflection, similar to the Lenten period before Easter. Advent does not play a very large role in the contemporary celebration of Christmas. Still, the belief persists that we must earn the indulgence of the holiday itself by undergoing a period of suffering and sacrifice. That is one of the purposes of the Christmas shopping season. Enduring the traffic, the crowds, the unresponsive salesclerks, and all the other irritants of the shopping season is the preparation we require to help make the holiday fully meaningful. The gusto with which people compete to tell the most harrowing holiday-shopping story demonstrates that the sacrifice of shopping is an essential part of the ultimate celebration.

This is true even though there are aspects of the holiday shopping season—the lights, the decorations, the special displays and shows, the windows with their animated scenes, the Salvation Army bands, even, sometimes, the crowds—that people clearly enjoy. Retailers know this, and they invest a lot of money in creating memorable holiday-shopping experiences. You can look at holiday shoppers and see that, while some are tense and driven, they look a lot happier than, for example, people who think they're having the time of their lives in gambling casinos. Yet the stories we tell of holiday shopping describe a series of disasters and a month-long ordeal. There is, however, a happy ending. Like Odysseus, we all come home in the end.

Inventing the American Christmas

It seems amazing, in light of the extravagance of the contemporary American Christmas, to realize that the country was founded mostly by people who didn't care much for holidays, and especially disliked Christmas. In the New England colonies and Pennsylvania, Puritans and Quakers opposed the holiday as idolatrous, or at least likely to contribute to self-destructive excess.

In England, from which most of the colonists came, the importance of the holiday had waxed and waned over the centuries. Primarily, it had been associated with the benevolence of the king, nobility, and gentry toward their lessers. King Henry III was known for having entertained a thousand knights and pages on Christmas at York, and he was later outdone by Richard II, who slew two thousand oxen and served two hundred barrels of wine for ten thousand guests. (One-fifth of an ox apiece seems like quite a lot.) Gift-giving consisted of expected benevolence from landowners. It was, in a sense, a reversal of usual feudal relationships, in which those lower in the social hierarchy regularly transferred wealth to their superiors. But it preserved the system as well, providing an escape valve for resentments and offering tokens to bolster the idea that the relationship between the landowners and the peasants had a bit of reciprocity about it. At Christmas, the peasants were able to get a taste of the fruits of their labors, the best the country could provide.

We have already seen how, with urbanization and the decline of feudalism, wealthier people spent more of their wealth on adorning and presenting themselves in London, and less on their expected benevolence. When they came to power, the Puritans outlawed Christmas, and even after the monarchy was restored, it was clear that the old feudal relationships around which the holiday was organized had been lost. In an increasingly urban culture, the idea of a long period of wintertime idleness, which was inevitable in the country, threatened productivity. As a result, the long winter festival largely disappeared.

In the United States in the early nineteenth century, there were very few widely celebrated holidays. Large parts of the country had been founded on the principle that Sunday is holiday enough, and the nation began without the array of saints' days and civic observances to be found in Europe. In the South, landowners were mostly Anglicans, who celebrated Christmas as some of the English gentry did, by offering lavish feasts. The English settlers of New York were predominantly Anglicans, so that was the city where Christmas was celebrated most publicly, though it was not a legally recognized holiday.

Among relatively prosperous city residents in the three decades after 1800, New Year's Day had been celebrated as a holiday, marked by giving open houses and visiting others, and to a lesser extent, by exchanging small gifts. The tradition of giving Christmas presents evolved from the Christmas box. This was an offering made by people of superior rank to servants, watchmen, newsboys, and others of lesser rank, on whom they depended for convenience and comfort. The custom derived from the medieval tradition of benevolence to the peasants. It survives today in the presents that are now expected by apartment-house doormen and superintendents, housekeepers and others in a servant role. The common assumption that these semicoerced presents were a latter-day, greedy innovation is wrong; in fact they are closer to the origins of the holiday than most of the traditions we view as sacrosanct. (There was also a tradition of giving small gifts to mummers who went from door to door to beg for them, a medieval vestige that often contained a threat.)

In 1823, Clement W. Moore, a wealthy New Yorker, published his poem "A Visit from Saint Nicholas," the source of much of the imagery of contemporary Christmas. We read it today as a description of an old-fashioned Christmas, but at the time, it was all quite new. The poem is based vaguely on a Dutch practice in which children put out their shoes on Saint Nicholas's Day, December 6, to be filled up with gifts. But the historian Stephen Nissenbaum says that there is absolutely no evidence that this tradition was ever practiced in New Amsterdam. Santa's coming down the chimney derives from the story of Saint Nicholas, bishop of Myra in what is now Turkey, who threw bags of gold through the windows (or down the chimney) of a poor family's house so the daughters would not have to become prostitutes. But Saint Nicholas had been a stern judgmental figure; Moore's saint was, above all, jolly.

This poem was a catalyst for redefining Christmas as a festival of the family, a domestic counterpart to the sociable New Year celebration. It celebrated the coming of a child, and it emphasized the nuclear-family unit of father, mother, and child. And this transformation could not have happened without the industrial revolution.

Industrialized societies produced more and cheaper goods to buy and to give, and, just as importantly, demographic changes that enabled Christmas to take root. The key to Christmas is the rise of the sheltered, middle-class family. In America, from about 1830 onward, the workplace and the home were increasingly defined as two entirely separate spheres. Young people, who had once worked alongside their parents (and still did in rural settings) were now sheltered from productivity; in Veblen's terms, they were a true leisure class. Meanwhile, the mother's role was to preside over this sphere and provide training, moral guidance, and a fit environment. As we have seen, shopping to provide for the material comforts and necessities of domesticity was defined as an important part of the woman's role.

Americans of the professional and business classes were having fewer children than their parents had. Indeed, in early-nineteenth-century magazines, advertisements for contraceptives and drugs to induce miscarriage were far more numerous than those advertising gift items for Christmas. Families consisting of fewer, more pampered children freed more parental time for enjoyment of children, who were now viewed not as economic assets but as enrichments of life. Mothers were seen as having a particular responsibility to see that their children would have good experiences. More money could be spent on each child as well. The elaborate hoax that is Santa Claus emerged from these smaller, more child-centered families. Christmas became a celebration of the beloved child in the sheltering home. This may or may not be the meaning of the swaddled infant in the manger in Bethlehem, but it has become the meaning of the American Christmas since the mid-nineteenth century.

Christmas has developed for the last century and a half as a holiday focused on children and run by women. Even in the religious tradition of Christmas, Joseph appears as something of a bystander. In the Gospels, he is pushed aside not only by the mother and child, but also by an exciting supporting cast of angels, shepherds, and wise men from the East. Joseph doesn't even have the status of being the baby's father. And in the contemporary celebration, Dad ends up playing second fiddle to Santa, the beloved provider of toys and other good things. (One of the enduring, late-nineteenth-century stereotyped scenes of Christmas is the decisive and acquisitive woman, striding confidently down the store aisle or shopping street, with her husband trailing behind, good for nothing but carrying a precariously balanced tower of parcels.)

Women were the primary creators of most of the traditions of Christmas, from decorating the home to putting up the tree and buying and wrapping the presents. These were all laborious tasks that, for the most part, they had to do themselves.

Even now that women are likely to have jobs outside the home,

Christmas is still viewed as women's work, by both men and women. In a 1990 study, researchers found that women start shopping earlier, buy far more presents, and spend less per gift. They feel more satisfied with how they perform at Christmas than men do, and see the holiday as a serious job that must be done well. Men more often see Christmas as a not-entirely-expected crisis that must somehow be endured. Women accept the burden of Christmas because, at least for now, most still accept their role as the makers of the family and the home.

It took several decades for this new kind of Christmas to emerge as the norm. Throughout the first half of the nineteenth century, many businesses remained open on Christmas; so many people did their Christmas shopping on Christmas Day that commercial streets in New York and Philadelphia were impassable. Although the periodicals and newspapers of the time point to no catalytic event, suddenly at midcentury, the climate changed and the news pages were filled with stories of women going to the stores to do their Christmas shopping. The women were also said to be making their own gifts and filling stockings for their children. This flurry of activity didn't seem to have been a marketer's plot, though retailers moved quickly to meet increasing demand. A few years later, there were accounts of taking children downtown to "see Christmas," as the buyosphere was suffused with imagery, some very ancient and much more that was newly invented, all of which served to make shopping for Christmas feel very different from the purchases made at other times of year.

There's no question that some retailers responded very quickly to the emerging interest in celebrating the Christmas season. In 1845, a Philadelphia store announced that Kris Kringle would be available to meet shoppers. A product of Pennsylvania's German tradition, Kris was different from Moore's Santa; he was thin, with sharp features, a tall hat, and a pointed beard. In 1874, Macy's filled its windows with $10,000 worth of dolls, and New Yorkers flocked to see them and do a little shopping besides. In 1920, Gimbel's created the Thanksgiving Day parade in Philadelphia to kick off the

Christmas season, an innovation quickly copied by Hudson's in Detroit and Macy's in New York. It's not entirely clear which retailer ran the first after-Christmas clearance sale, but that, too, has become an important part of the ritual that accounts for a large share of holiday spending.

Still, it is interesting that even as late as the 1880s, retailers' trade publications were still admonishing shopkeepers to make special preparations for the Christmas season by ordering stock geared to the holiday, and creating displays and events to make their stores part of the celebration.

We often assume that the commercial Christmas we know was a fall from grace from a traditional religious holiday, but in fact, the secular and commercial holiday evolved simultaneously. For example, nearly all the Christmas carols we still sing today were either written or rendered into English between 1850 and 1870. And they were popularized, in part, by merchants such as John Wanamaker, who distributed thousands of Christmas hymnals for free to shoppers each holiday season. Some churches had long been hostile to Christmas celebrations and were forced to respond to the demands of their parishioners.

Many other Christmas traditions that we now accept as given started relatively modestly. The Christmas tree has deep roots in Northern European tree worship. Queen Victoria and Prince Albert imported the German tradition of the Christmas tree to England, and increased its popularity in America, where it had already been introduced by immigrants from Germany. Victoria and Albert's tree was small enough to stand on a tabletop. For a long time, Christmas presents were hung on Christmas trees, often in small paper cornucopias, which had been manufactured for that purpose. That meant Christmas presents were rather small and light in weight. Not until the end of the nineteenth century did presents begin to greatly outgrow the carrying capacities of spruce trees—and of hosiery hanging from fireplace mantels—and move into wrapped and decorated boxes instead.

The wrapping of Christmas presents is a topic that has been of particular interest to anthropologists and folklore scholars. It caught on after stores began using inexpensive boxes that were easy to wrap, but why the etiquette of gift-wrapping arose is still unclear. Nowadays, just about all presents are wrapped, except those that are just too huge or awkward to wrap, or items that are homemade, especially cakes or cookies, which are usually adorned with only a bow or a piece of yarn.

Some anthropologists have speculated that the act of wrapping is an attempt to disguise the industrial and commercial origins of the presents, and thus, in a sense, to decontaminate them. This is not a wholly convincing argument, especially since present-givers rarely make any effort to disguise where they obtained the present.

It seems more likely that wrapping is meant as a sign of caring. The wrap adds a personal and handmade element to a mass-produced product. The wrapping is not a disguise; it is tangible evidence that the giver thought about the recipient. It signals that the gift is really part of a personal relationship.

But there is also something more. The wrapping makes the gift into a Christmas decoration. The holiday, as it arose in the nineteenth century, celebrated the sheltering home, and it still does. Once, the presents decorated the tree. When they proliferated and grew in size, they were gathered beneath the tree. Everyone who brings a present contributes to the collective expression of the household and the family. The tree and its wrapped presents become the household's most important piece of holiday décor. True, when the presents are opened, they become personal property rather than part of a collective expression, but, at least momentarily, the display of brightly wrapped presents offers a compelling symbol of family unity.

Santa Claus: Indulgence and self-control

Santa Claus is the central character of our commercial Christmas, and for many he is a troubling one. Does he primarily serve the purpose of indoctrinating children to be greedy for consumer goods, starting an addiction that will last the rest of their lives? Or is Santa Claus good for children, helping them both to celebrate a special time and to achieve a measure of self-control?

Santa Claus and his counterparts have always been a source of concern to the religious. Because he is understood to be omniscient and a source of blessings, he is a child's version of a god. Indeed, he still resembles Saturn, the Roman god whose holiday once dominated the season. But he is a businesslike demigod, one who has many of the accoutrements of a nineteenth-century peddler. In the twentieth century, he morphed into a more serious sort of businessman, operator of both an offshore factory at the North Pole manned by elf labor, and of the world's most efficient overnight delivery service.

Thus, Santa's enemies see him as a blasphemous figure who lures the smallest children into a pseudo-religion of marketplace idolatry and makes our society the morally bankrupt, materially wasteful spiritual desert it is.

On the other hand, despite his godlike characteristics, Santa is not defined as a religious figure; his magic is wholly nonsectarian. Americans may differ over their religious doctrine, but the idea of a miracle-worker who bestows grace in the form of brand-name merchandise is something we can all agree upon.

The best defense of Santa Claus came from the anthropologist Claude Lévi-Strauss. He argued that Santa Claus (actually his French counterpart, Père Noel) helps children learn to discipline themselves. This is, first of all, because the degree of Santa's benevolence is said to be directly proportional to the children's good behavior. (He sees you when you're sleeping, after all.) Perhaps more importantly, Lévi-Strauss writes, "Giving presents only at a certain time is a useful way of disciplining children's demands, reducing to a brief period the time when children have the right to demand presents."

More or less the same argument could be made for the whole Christmas season. It channels a large part of our expenditures and our indulgence into a celebration of useful, if sometimes problematic institutions—the home and family. It concentrates spending in a short period of time, and it may even help some people practice thrift during much of the rest of the year, if only because their credit cards are maxed out.

Contemporary retailers do all they can to get their maximum return from Christmas; they have little choice. But concentrating so large a percentage of traffic and revenues into a short season means that shoppers face congestion, retailers field untrained temporary help, and large amounts of inventory must be stocked with little sense of what will sell. These difficulties were already evident during the last third of the nineteenth century, when the holiday shopping festival took shape. That's why some retailers resisted committing themselves fully to the stock-planning, extra staff, decorations, special events, and big business risks involved in the season. Contemporary retailers make nearly all their profits in the fourth quarter of the year. Many carry debt through much of the year, to be paid off after the holidays. For them, the holiday shopping season is a gamble that can always be lost. Shoppers sometimes feel that Christmas is a conspiracy by the stores, the malls, and the Main Streets, but in fact, few retailers would, if they could start over, design a system in which so much of their business depends on such a small part of the year.

For more than a century, retailers have tried to cope with the extreme demands of the season in several ways. One is to encourage early shopping by increasing the length of the holiday season. This was originally presented to the public as a way of being kind to overworked store clerks, but now early shopping is presented as a mark of efficiency, an attribute of the smart shopper. Strategic shoppers, though, will save at least some shopping to the end, in the hope of picking up some bargains. In any case, this longer shopping season never succeeded in avoiding the last-minute crunch, and it certainly contributes to the phenomenon of shopping burnout and the perception that the holiday has been excessively commercialized.

The other strategy has been to establish other occasions for exchanging gifts in order to spread out the traffic, spending, and cash flow. In Japan, for example, there is a midsummer gift season that balances off the New Year's gift season, but in North America and Europe, nothing so compelling has emerged. For many years, Easter was associated with renewal and new spring wardrobes, but that holiday has, during the last half-century, become a far less important public celebration than it once was. It seems that as it has lost its religious significance, it has also lost its commercial power. Many other three-day weekends, such as Presidents' Day, Labor Day, and Memorial Day have become occasions for sales, and particular stores have long had a full calendar of specialized sales to draw people in. The late-summer back-to-school period is the only other lengthy shopping season, though it doesn't hold a candle to Christmas.

One of the familiar platitudes of the holidays is that it's too bad that their spirit can't be felt at other times. From a shopper's standpoint, it's more likely that the opposite is true. Christmas comes but once a year, and that is its virtue. It is a difficult time, a nerve-wracking time, an extraordinary time, a season for giving and indulging. We could never afford to have it last all year long.

9
CONVENIENCE
Efficiency, Branding, and the Tangled Lives of Shoppers

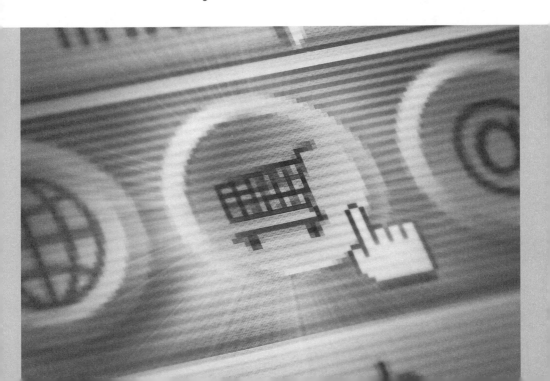

*W*hen she found out about this book, my friend Anita wanted to make sure that it included an account of what she called "the old kind of shopping." By that she meant the kind of shopping her mother did, and the kind that she learned to do during the 1950s, when she was in her teens.

"Shopping was an occasion," she says. "You didn't do it all the time, but when you did it, it was serious." Her recollections revolve around a famous, now closed, specialty store where many generations of upper-class women bought their dresses and accessories. It was the sort of store where you had your own saleswoman, one you may well have inherited from others in your family. And if you were a good customer, she would always be on the lookout for items that might suit you.

"She would want to know about the occasion for wearing the dress," Anita recalls; some of her other customers had probably purchased frocks for the same event. "And she had a discreet, indirect way of finding out how much I—or my mother—was willing to spend. She would bring out the dresses one by one, and point out the material and the style." Anita and her mother were seated in a private room. Occasionally, Anita would try on a dress.

"You might spend an hour doing this, and never see a thing you liked," she says. "But the saleslady always had something in reserve. Just as we were about to give up and leave, she would pull out something special. It would always cost a little bit more than we wanted to spend, though not too much more. For some reason, it always seemed to be exactly what I had in mind. And though the price was high, it looked so much better on me than those other things I tried that it seemed to be worth the price.

"I think that that was the dress she meant to sell me all along," Anita says. "Those other dresses were there to make that one seem wonderful. Even at the time, I understood what she was doing, but I enjoyed the experience." And she enjoys the memory.

Still, Anita, who is a time-pressed businesswoman, would not sit still for such an experience today. Like most working women, she prefers to go to stores that offer a good selection of the brands, styles, and designers she likes. She expects to follow her own path toward the right dress, rather than expect someone else to lead her there.

In retrospect, the old-style service seems leisurely, but it was also very convenient. The saleslady knew her customers and, even more importantly, their friends; she could make a very good judgment about what clothes to wear. Today, such service is no longer useful because Anita is living in a larger world where she demands a different sort of convenience. For her, as for most contemporary shoppers, finding the right item at a good price is the best service a store can offer. "That was selling as an art," she says of the salesclerk of her youth. "But who has time for that nowadays?"

Now that women are typically working outside of the household, the formal, female-organized social calendar that induced Anita's seemingly leisurely but serious shopping is largely a memory. Work life, social life, and family life are seriously tangled. Instead of a handful of special events, there are now countless moments when it is important to present yourself and members of your family in a good light. Shopping is just as necessary, but serves other agendas. "I want my dress to signal that I am someone with authority," said one woman executive quoted in a 1997 study, "so that they will know that my 'no' is a 'no!'" Another said she wants her clothing to communicate to people she doesn't know "that I'm going to care about them and they can trust me to do something for them."

Shopping has to compete with a lot of other demands on people's time. Many women tell market survey–takers that their idea of a satisfying leisure activity consists of tranquil private moments, when they feel that their time is their own. It is less and less likely to involve trying on dresses at the mall.

This trend suggests that shopping needs to become easier and faster. Stores need to become more efficient in identifying their markets, editing their stock, telling people where things can be found. Catalogues, the Internet, and television shopping channels provide opportunities to save time by shopping at home or during breaks at work. Most of the time, shopping is not seen as a special event, but as something that can happen any time, all the time. Just as a woman may be always a mother, always a wife, always a lawyer, so she is always a shopper.

This plea for greater efficiency in shopping conflicts with a different reality, that shopping is often a leisure activity—one of the most popular of all pastimes. There's no doubt that it's a leisure activity by Veblen's definition; people don't produce anything when they shop. For a significant minority of the population, shopping fits a broader definition of leisure: it is something that people do for fun, for recreation, or because they can't think of an alternative way of spending their time.

The contradiction between the goals of efficiency and leisure diminishes a bit when we consider that people in contemporary society are leading tangled lives. Work interrupts private life. Sales pitches interrupt everything. There seems to be little time for parenting, so shopping is being recast as an opportunity for the family to be together.

This drive to transform shopping into a form of family entertainment is, in fact, an attempt to adapt shopping to contemporary living patterns. The thrust of retail innovation throughout the last century has been to create new sorts of convenience for the shopper: new kinds of stores and shopping environments such as regional malls, power centers, and the Internet; making shopping more predictable by branding both goods and retail experiences and establishing a more varied, and essentially inescapable, buyosphere. Convenience is not simply about the efficiency of finding and acquiring merchandise. It is making shoppers feel comfortable and receptive. It is about respecting shoppers and responding to their needs. Perhaps most important of all, it is about recognizing that people have a lot more to do in their lives, besides shopping.

$\mathcal{R}$edefining convenience

As we have seen, ever since shopping first arose in sixteenth-century Europe, there have been city districts where merchants and artisans offering similar goods have clustered together. The same thing happened 2,400 years ago in the Athens agora. The disadvantage of being next door to your competitors is that if you fail to match their price and quality, you will suffer. But the overwhelming advantage is that shoppers looking for a particular item will know exactly where to look.

For a long time, such thinking was anathema to managers of large shopping malls. It was considered poor planning to place stores that sold similar or overlapping lines of goods next to one another. The idea was to force someone who wanted to compare styles and prices of a pair of dress shoes or a set of sheets to trudge through the entire mall. The hope was that she would pass stores offering a silk scarf or a bottle of bath salts, items she might not have intended to buy but that are, nevertheless, irresistible. A few mall operators have begun to realize that the edge they have over other retail venues is that they offer multiple sellers of similar goods so that those who really intend to buy can compare. They have begun to create districts within their malls, where stores selling furniture, housewares, business apparel, or women's shoes are clustered to create a convenient shopping experience. This is not yet common practice, but innovations that work in one mall tend to be adopted very rapidly everywhere.

Mall operators have been forced to adapt because, throughout the 1990s, consumers began to seek out shopping alternatives that they found more convenient. Huge malls, where you must park far away and spend time getting to scattered destinations, have come to feel too onerous, an investment of time and energy that contemporary shoppers feel they cannot afford. One alternative was the creation of strip centers—rows of stores with parking lots—whose retailers specialize, for example, in home decoration and renovation. One store might offer furniture and lighting, another dishware and furniture, yet another storage supplies and bedding, and there is overlap so the shopper can compare items from two or more retailers. By combining one-stop shopping with quick-stop shopping, such centers help answer a contemporary call for convenience.

Other alternatives to the mall include big box stores, such as Wal-Mart, Kmart, and Target, which offer a comprehensive assortment of products, some of them exclusive and smartly designed. There are also strip centers that consist entirely of "category killers," specialized chains that dominate a product line or market segment. The ultimate category killer is Toys"R"Us, which so dominates its industry that department stores and many malls don't even bother to compete. Another, Home Depot, has made the hardware store obsolete.

Yet there can be too much of a good thing. Some shoppers find bliss getting lost amid Home Depot's shower heads, hinges, and replacement windows, while others find it a vision of hell.

Do shoppers want to find exactly what they are looking for, or do they want to get lost? This is an age-old question, and the answer of course is that they like to do both, and nearly all stores and shopping districts mix the two impulses. Even supermarkets, which are rigorously classified and labeled, nevertheless offer mid-aisle and aisle-end displays that break up the order and try to tempt shoppers to stray from, or at least augment, their intentions. In department stores, the balance between order and chaos helps define the store's character.

For example, nearly a century ago, John Wanamaker recognized that many of his shoppers were working women who needed to get in and out quickly, so he offered a very clearly organized store. Today, all outlets of Kohl's, a discount department-store chain, are laid out in a single-floor racetrack pattern. This makes it easier for shoppers to get in, find what they want quickly, and see a lot of other products besides. This space-efficient, time-efficient scheme produces high revenue per square foot, which is the way retailers measure their success.

Yet other department-store chains have been very successful with configurations that were intentionally confusing. During the 1970s and early 1980s, the New York–based Bloomingdale's chain created stores that were intentionally mazelike. Sightlines were limited, paths were circuitous, and one encountered the same merchandise in many places, often among goods to which they had no logical relationship. Yet Bloomingdale's was convenient in its way because it seemed to be a one-stop opportunity for the affluent, young, childless consumers the store called "Saturday's generation" to find the clothes and furnishings of their lifestyle.

Surprise is one of the things we hope to find when we shop. And store owners make big profits from the things we didn't intend to buy. It's not likely, therefore, that our stores and malls will ever be organized according to any sort of Dewey decimal system. It does seem likely, though, that in an era when most people claim to feel that they have no time, shopping needs to be made easier and less stressful. And that means, either in a store or on a Web site, making it easier for people to find both what they want *and* what they can't resist.

Filene's Basement and the self-assured, self-service shopper

At the turn of the twentieth century, Boston's Filene's, like most big department stores, was a family-owned business. Unlike most of their counterparts, however, the Filene family had a great interest in understanding retailing not as an art but as a science. On most of the floors of the store, salesclerks were instructed to suppress their opinions and underestimate their customers' sizes. The woman's role in the bourgeois household was to set the standards of culture and taste for her family. The department stores accepted her, and showed her how.

Filene's, like most department stores, also had a bargain store in its basement to sell cheaper or discontinued items. Much of the clientele consisted of people who could not afford to shop upstairs, but some of the basement shoppers were carrying out an obligation of the middle-class wife: to obtain goods for her family at a reasonable cost. Status was fine as far as it went, but a bargain was even better. The point was not to buy cheaply, but to pay less for items of quality and taste.

In 1909, Filene's made a major innovation in its basement. It began to stock a larger quantity of the higher-quality items that shoppers might, a few months before, have found upstairs or at other top stores. And it instituted an automatic markdown system that drastically cut the price of an item after a certain number of days on the racks. All pretense of gentility was cast aside. The shopper was on her own, with only her own taste, eye for quality, and aggressiveness to rely upon.

The automatic markdown feature, which survives in the original Boston store, is, in Internet parlance, sticky. It encourages shoppers to come back again and again, to see what's new and to check to see whether particular items are still there after the next markdown kicks in. It also encourages such guerrilla shopping tactics as moving an item to the wrong location, in the hope that competitive shoppers won't find it before markdown day. The system creates the sense of scarcity that makes people want to buy. It turns shopping into a meaningful game: getting things for less than they are "worth." The shopper becomes both a hunter and a gatherer, Filene's Basement a Kalahari wilderness experience in contemporary terms.

Filene's Basement was not the beginning of self-service; most bargain stores and some areas of quality department and specialty stores had that. But it was one of the earliest arenas for the smart, independent shopper, the sort of person who relied on her own discernment, was confident of her taste, and didn't need anyone to mediate between herself and the goods. Today, of course, this description fits most shoppers most of the time. But early in the twentieth century, most retailers felt shoppers needed assistance, and they didn't like the idea of shoppers rummaging through the merchandise and ruining it. Now, because styles change so rapidly that many items lose their premium status quickly, shoppers expect to see everything available, and because sales help is an expense, just about all retailers take that risk.

Self-service retailing was relatively slow to catch on. Five-and-ten-cent stores offered minimal sales assistance, but they still kept most of their items in cases. Grocery stores only began to experiment with self-service retailing during the 1920s. The first supermarkets opened in the 1930s, though they did not become ubiquitous until after 1945. Department stores kept a lot of stock on open display, so that shoppers could browse quickly and inspect items that interested them. But clerks were at hand, ready to assist the shopper in examining and perhaps trying on the item.

Self-service for garments, linens, housewares, and small appliances came only during the 1950s, as part of the second phase of post–World War II suburbanization, after much of the middle class had moved from the cities and shopping began to follow. The first retailers to colonize the strip centers adjacent to bedroom neighborhoods were discount houses, which followed the now-familiar model of the supermarket. Every shopper had a cart. They picked up the item they sought, put it into the cart, and brought it to the checkout counter. Such stores were less expensive. They were close to home. And they were easy to use. The absence of clerks reduced the personal friction that could sometimes discourage sales. The shopper bonded directly with the item, and she pushed it out the door and into the car.

Eventually, the downtown department stores, which had made

tentative forays into the suburbs as early as the 1920s, realized that virtually all shopping had migrated to where people lived. And in the 1960s, they began to open branches in large regional shopping centers, which quickly metamorphosed into enclosed malls, where they were surrounded by smaller chain stores that developers had discovered contributed to a profitable mix. Indeed, big-performing little stores provide the developers' profit margins. Department stores in malls typically pay low rents; developers need them to generate traffic.

This is familiar story that will not be belabored here. Usually, this displacement and transformation of shopping is attributed to the automobile, and with good reason. Suburbia as we know it wouldn't be possible without the car. And in the United States, policies of the post–World War II era that encouraged the spread of suburbia were instituted for the very purpose of encouraging spending. The idea was that new larger houses outside of cities would induce more spending on automobiles, furnishings, appliances, and other goods. This purchasing, the theory went, would prevent the economy from falling back into the depression that had blighted the 1930s. Americans bought into this idea, big-time, and we have kept on moving out into subdivisions in the country, purchasing more and bigger cars and larger houses, even though hardly anybody remembers the Great Depression. Indeed, many of the houses that seemed so airy and sprawling in the post–World War II era are now viewed as small and spartan. They face the threat of being torn down to make room for larger houses.

$\mathcal{D}$emigods in the aisles: The rise of brand shopping

But the car and the suburb are not the only forces that shaped the modern era of self-service shopping. The declining authority of the store and its representative the salesclerk is almost entirely the result of the increasing authority of the brand. No matter what they are buying, today's shoppers arrive at the store with a clear idea of the characteristics, the quality, and the meanings of hundreds, or even thousands, of branded products.

We think of brands somewhat as we think of our friends, though perhaps more as a polytheist thought of his gods. They have strengths and attributes, but weaknesses too. As with the Greek gods, their usefulness depends on the situation. If you're fighting cockroaches, you want a product that's strong and shows no mercy, but nobody will buy Raid toothpaste.

While our great-grandmothers might have been swayed by the palatial architecture of a great downtown department store, we stand in the same place, look at the item and its label, and know that we can buy it for eight dollars less at the outlet mall on the edge of town.

Branded products are not new; the Romans had a few. Patent medicines and grooming products started to appear in sixteenth-century London, and some relatively familiar names, such as Cadbury's and Wedgwood, survive from the eighteenth century. But the great age of branding began just before the turn of the twentieth century. It was made possible by advances in packaging, in color printing, and by the maturing of nationwide transportation and communications networks.

As we have seen, the department store and the metropolitan newspaper grew up together and reflected each other. They were both tied to a particular place, in which each served as a source for nearly everything the world offered. Brands aren't tied to a particular region, or even to a particular store. They are best served by national media, first of all national magazines, then later, and even more powerfully, radio and television. For nearly a century, brand advertising has underwritten much of the news and entertainment the American household receives. In the process, the home, which was redefined in the early nineteenth century as a refuge from the world of money and manufacture, became the number-one commercial target.

Nowadays, we spend our days bombarded with commercial messages in private settings and consider it normal. Brand imagery is our modern mythology, and we learn it mostly at home. During the 1920s, however, when radio was first becoming widespread, this was a sensitive issue. Radio was a new and potentially disturbing voice in the home, and at least at first, those in the industry felt an obligation to tread lightly. "The family circle is not a public place," *Printers' Ink*, the advertising industry magazine, declared in 1923, "and advertising has no business intruding there unless it is invited." The radio and advertising industries worked hard to make sure that such advertising was welcomed as a guest, rather than an unwelcome peddler with his foot wedged in the door. For nearly a century, the home had been seen as a refuge from the world of commerce. Magazines and mail-order catalogues had, to be sure, established a beachhead of the buyosphere in the home, but these were seen and not heard. Radio was far more intrusive, and in its early years, advertisers worried that radio commercials might alienate as many listeners as they convinced.

By the late 1920s, however, radio was thoroughly commercialized, and advertisers were producing many of its most popular programs. Product packaging, which had long been called "the silent salesman," was joined by a new kind of salesman, radio, which never shut up. During the Great Depression, even though most people were unable to buy much, radio helped sustain the dream of shopping and extol the magic of having. Victims of the Depression never became as angry as many commentators feared or hoped they would. Very likely it was because people believed in their brands.

When families decided to welcome radio and, later, television advertising into their homes in exchange for a steady diet of information and entertainment, the nature of household life changed. It used to be that people went out to shop for things they brought home. Now, much of every day is filled with instructions on how to shop. Shopping is no longer a discrete activity, but a matter for consideration for several minutes every half hour. And even the programming, which helps define how people dress and live, leads us into commercial temptation. Shopping may not be exactly a leisure activity, but such leisure activities as listening to the radio, watching television, or even participating in an Internet chat room are filled with advice on how to shop. Indeed, one of the chief challenges of Internet-based retailing is to make its advertising intrusive enough to be noticed, without making it so obnoxious that it will alienate potential customers.

The firm establishment of brand names by the 1930s is what made the first supermarkets possible. If shoppers could see that a cut-rate seller like New York's pioneering King Kullen was selling exactly the same national brands as the local grocery, there was good reason to travel a little farther to get a better price. This was the beginning of a long deterioration of the authority of retailers as definers of style and quality, and the concomitant rise of packaged, advertised, branded products that could be found at a variety of outlets.

Branding changed the retail landscape by making individual stores less special, and by making self-service the norm. And the tools that build brands, preeminently advertising, change the psychological landscape as well. Even if you don't spend a lot of time shopping, you do spend a lot of time preparing for it, whether you want to do so or not.

Branding offers real advantages for shoppers. It promises uniform standards of quality. It lets us know what we can expect. It gives goods an identity, and helps us understand how we should feel about them. On a more practical level, branding is a great sorting and time-saving mechanism. When faced with a store that has tens of thousands of different items, we use the brands to help make decisions quickly.

This time-saving aspect of brands has only grown more important during the last three decades, as large numbers of women have joined the workforce. Shopping must fit into increasingly busy lives. Shoppers have coped with time restraints by relying on familiar brands for everything from scouring powder to business attire. "Designer labels," after all, are not really about design, they are about branding. Often the same label is found on perfume, sheets, blue jeans, wallpaper, furniture, sweatshirts, and business clothes for both men and women. In survey after survey, shoppers have told researchers that a good store is one that sells trusted brands at low prices. (Increasingly, though, people have shown a willingness to purchase "quality" fakes of well-known brands. In a 2000 British survey, 40 percent said they would do so, though they were far more likely to purchase fake clothing than something that had to work well, such as electronic equipment. We do buy things to impress others, and sometimes take shortcuts.)

*B*randed entertainment and shopping for fun

Today, what appear to be the highest-profile shopping and entertainment experiences—on Michigan Boulevard in Chicago, Rodeo Drive in Beverly Hills, or Fifth Avenue in New York—are actually branding experiences. These can be stores of high-end retailers, such as Gucci or Louis Vuitton, or showcases for mass-market products, such as Sony or Nike.

Attractions such as Niketown draw people from long distances because, like the great stores of old, they provide a compelling context for the goods they offer. By contrast, most mall retailing has a generic feeling, which isn't surprising. When you repeat the same formula for the five-hundredth time, it's bound to feel a little tired. Niketown stands out among contemporary retail experiences because it has been designed with such careful attention to detail. Its purpose is not so much to sell shoes as to sell a way of moving, feeling, and being that can't happen without the shoes. Every square inch is ornamented. Each part of the building has its own subtle sound, its own light, its own texture. As in a Gothic cathedral, there seems to be more meaning here than one can possibly take in at one time. Still, visitors seem delighted to figure out, for example, that the pattern on the "manhole covers" that decorate the floor alludes to the waffle-patterned soles of the first Nikes. Nikephiles know that these soles were actually made on a waffle iron. Going to Niketown is almost like embarking on a commercial pilgrimage place, and as at Chartres, if you know the myths being celebrated, you will enjoy the experience even more. Marketing takes it a step farther: When you go to the discount store where you actually buy your footware, the aura of the brand will endure.

Niketown feels like a fragment of a theme park. The two largest malls in North America—in West Edmonton, Alberta, and Bloomington, Minnesota—have theme parks at their center. One of the most successful retail developments in recent years is in Caesars Palace in Las Vegas, a casino hotel which is, itself, largely a theme park. Universal's City Walk development gives Los Angeles the sort of intimate, nostalgic strolling environment that most people believe the city has never had. In New York's Times Square, an entertainment center has replaced the more tawdry elements with branded attractions and entertainment-retail hybrids, and billions of dollars' worth of new value has been created.

Some real-estate developers and entrepreneurs have looked at these success stories and concluded that the old mall formula is exhausted. There need to be attractions that will lure all members of the family to the mall and keep them there. The future of shopping, they argue, is entertainment.

Shopping-center operators, retailers, and entertainment companies have been trying, in recent years, to transform every shopping trip into an entertainment event, an escape from everyday life. The theory is that customers will have fewer inhibitions and be willing to spend more on conventional items. And they will be willing to pay something for the experience, hence the entertainment component of these retail complexes. The amusements also encourage dad and the children to come along, eating more and spending freely on a family outing. This new shopping paradigm goes by the buzzwords "shoputainment," or "location-based entertainment."

In some ways, this is a very old idea. In early-nineteenth-century England, some shopping bazaars showed menageries of exotic animals. In doing so, they merely carried on the tradition of the great fairs, which also featured menageries and all sorts of traveling acrobats, magicians, singers, and actors. London's famous Bartholomew Fair, itself the subject of a play by Ben Jonson that satirized Puritans, had become by the fifteenth century almost entirely song, drink, and bawdy jokes. It was a disreputable event that was also, some have argued, the wellspring of the English theater.

Today's shopping-related entertainment is unlikely to produce a Shakespeare. For the most part it consists of expensive, elaborate virtual-reality games, and places where young people can skateboard. It also encompasses restaurants, such as the Rainforest Café, that offer a unique environment, and even a bit of idealism, along with the food.

However, some operators are taking the idea a bit further. One concept that has been tested during the last few years is the American Wilderness Experience, or AWE, whose slogan is "Go wild at the mall." It mixes exhibits of actual native wildlife, such as hawks, snakes, and beavers, with an amusement-park ride that offers an eagle's-eye view of different biological habitats. (The old-fashioned menageries had lions, bears, and other charismatic megafauna that cannot be accommodated humanely in a mall.) There are also, of course, a place to buy souvenirs, and a place to eat. This is sold as a destnation for a family outing, though its location in an outlet shopping mall suggests that it is a place to park one's husband and kids while hunting for bargains.

The idea behind theming the mall is a simple one. People spend more when they are on vacation. According to a 2000 travel-industry study, the average tourist spends $333 shopping while on vacation, and one in five spends more than $500. The same study suggested that people travel in order to shop, often citing it ahead of sightseeing as the reason to travel. Going away frees shoppers from their inhibitions, and opens their eyes to novelty. Moreover, it is convenient for people to buy things when they are away from home because they are freed from many routine obligations. This has been true to some degree at least since the days of the great medieval fairs, but travel industry statistics show that shopping is increasingly coming to dominate vacations. Thus, it's no mystery that retailers want to encourage shoppers to feel that they can take a half-day vacation every Saturday.

So far, though, the entertainment attractions have not been the surefire successes their promoters foresaw. That's especially true of the more elaborate ones that need constantly to be unveiling new attractions in order to get people to visit a second time. And even movie multiplexes, which were added to hundreds of malls during the 1990s, have not greatly increased mall traffic. Instead, their proliferation has driven several of the largest cinema-operating companies into bankruptcy.

Vacations are times when we give ourselves permission to spend. In that sense, they are like Christmas. But just as we can't make every encounter with our families into Christmas, we can't make every trip to the mall into a vacation. People shop during their leisure time; a handful of people spend nearly all their vacations doing nothing else, and many more shop when they're relaxing. But shopping is not *just* a leisure activity. It is too important for that.

Convenience in an atmosphere of divided attention

Because brands offer familiarity and reassurance, they allow shoppers to make decisions quickly. Brands flourish amid divided attention, a problem that has beset those trying to provide for their families since hunter-gatherer times. It may be that the deliberation with which Anita was able to approach her selection of a new dress was a historical exception; most of the time, people have met their needs while trying to accomplish something else. And that is certainly true today.

The idea of the home as shelter from the world has long since been shattered by radio, television, telephones, long working hours, the Internet, and many of the other fixtures of modern life. A century ago, Thorstein Veblen was able to divide human activity into manufacturing and consumption, and life as a whole into work and leisure. Now, few people in developed countries ever *make* anything, but we are all busier than ever, mostly gathering and collating information, and trying to get one another organized. Many of us spend our lives manipulating symbols, but our own careers can depend on how others see the things we buy and the things we wear. Sometimes, perhaps, we shop to relax, but just as often, we shop to succeed.

Home is no refuge from the commercial world, nor is it any longer a refuge from the world of work. When we go hiking in the woods, the mobile phone comes along, justified as a safety measure. But it also represents the likelihood of interruption, the impossibility of escape. When we head off to Eden nowadays, we carry our own snakes.

Work is tangled up with family; doing is tangled up with buying. If you feel that there is no time to shop, you probably also feel that you don't have time to get your job done, don't have time to be a good parent, lover, athlete, reader, or couch potato. Everything interrupts everything else.

A recent article in *Network World*, a trade magazine for those who manage business computer systems, provides a glimpse of the new shapes our lives are taking. It addresses a controversy that has emerged in the workplace: Should workers be allowed to do Christmas shopping on their computers at work? Some of the objections to the practice deal with such technical matters as network security, but the main one is the presumed loss of productivity, both of the computer system and the employees who use it. This is understandable. At least since the coming of the industrial revolution, we have expected to produce on the job, and consume on our own time.

But the author of this article, Jason Meserve, argues that we shouldn't fall into such old-economy thinking. Allowing people to take a few minutes out to shop might actually raise productivity. "While I am shopping online," he writes, "I am sitting at my desk where I can answer phone calls and e-mail and speak with anyone that stops by to talk about work. If I am at the mall, none of this is possible. Granted, I could go to the mall after work, but that would mean I couldn't stay late to deal with work that needs to be completed."

In other words, the danger of denying people the opportunity to shop is that they might actually leave the office. (About one-quarter of those who work on computers report that they shop at least once a month at work, including during lunch hours and other breaks.)

Unlike the Department of Labor, Meserve assumes that there are ten to twelve hours in a typical working day, and for those he is discussing, he may well be right. Several economists have theorized that the massive increase in productivity that the United States experienced during the 1990s resulted from large numbers of people working hours for which they were not paid.

To some extent, Meserve's argument appears humane, but it is also exploitative, a way of keeping employees under tight control. It certainly calls into question the old social contract, which stipulates that going out and buying things is the reward for doing our work. Now, according to the gurus of the new economy, we are expected to spend our money during brief lulls in the business day. There is no grandeur, no fantasy, no discovery in that. Such shopping may be efficient. But it doesn't feel like an achievement. And it doesn't feel like fun.

The word "convenience" comes from Latin roots that mean "coming together." This coming together should be a confluence of opportunity, obligation, and desire. It should be a smooth connection, not an anxiety-producing snarl. Often, what is intended to be a convenience can easily turn into its opposite, an unwelcome intrusion into our lives, a trap in which it is all too easy to get tangled.

Just as Anita's definition of convenience changed along with her own life and needs, the entire idea of convenience keeps being redefined, as habits, technologies, and expectations change.

The key for anyone who wants to introduce convenience into shopping is to remember the emotions that give rise to shopping. People want to feel powerful and to exercise responsibility. They want to discover things and to explore how they can re-create themselves. Shopping need not always be entertaining. And it should certainly be escapable. Our lives may feel tangled, but shopping must be what it has always been: a practical expression of freedom.

AFTERWORD
The Future of Shopping

*W*hen I began this book, not so long ago, all shopping seemed poised to disappear into the Internet. With the same rhetoric of inevitability with which some once talked about Communism, people discussed how shopping the Web would change every facet of life as we know it.

Retailers with legendary names, loyal customers, and proven ability to change with the times were valued far less than start-up Internet businesses with only a vague idea, a confusing Web site, and a business strategy that called for losing money on each item sold. Part of the reason I decided to write this book was that I felt the Internet boom was missing some fundamental points about human behavior. And it was about to make some of the same mistakes many others had made before.

One of my favorite specimens of this hubris was a "Manager's Journal" column on the editorial page of the *Wall Street Journal,* April 10, 2000, not long after Priceline.com announced launching of Web-House, a subsidiary to sell groceries and gasoline. The idea was that shoppers would submit a bid for the supermarket item they desired—laundry detergent, for example—though not for a specific brand like Tide or All. If the bid was accepted, the item could be picked up at a nearby supermarket.

I thought this was madness. Who wants to work so hard to purchase every single grocery item? I wondered. When you have to concentrate on each purchase, you're going to buy less. This didn't seem a formula for commercial success.

Besides, people feel strongly about the brands they want. I might be pleased with Tide or All, but do I want to settle for Dynamo or Fab? When people use discount coupons as an opportunity to sample new brands, it's a positive act. But why should grocery manufacturers offer similar subsidies to shoppers who will only be disappointed because they failed to obtain what they were hoping for?

Clay Shirky, the *Journal*'s writer, felt differently. "Priceline's new offering is a harbinger of a revolution being wrought by the information economy: the disappearance of fixed retail prices," he predicted. Fixed prices, he argued, were an unintended consequence of the industrial revolution. "Textbook economics," he wrote, "says fluid prices are the most efficient way to balance supply and demand." Through most of history, he added, haggling has been the rule of commerce, and computers and the Internet had once again made it efficient.

It must be an exciting thing for an economist to see the real world behave like an economics textbook—if only because it happens so rarely. This particular revolution lasted fewer than six months. WebHouse went out of business, killed by consumers who didn't want to cope with uncertainty, and manufacturers who didn't want to devalue their brands.

WebHouse was an economically and technologically sophisticated idea that was psychologically stupid. In the Middle Ages, for which Shirky seemed nostalgic, most people bought relatively few things. Today, we buy many things. The optimum price of each item is less important than the sense that we're shopping responsibly and getting good bargains. How do we know if we're getting a bargain if there are no fixed prices?

What an economist calls "fluidity" is experienced by real people as anxiety. Anxiety about whether you'll get the product before it runs out can help sales. But anxiety over whether you're paying too much—the anxiety that comes from haggling—does precisely the opposite.

Predictions of the technological transformation of shopping seem to be based on two major assumptions. One is that people are willing and eager to keep buying things during every waking moment. The other is that people hate to shop. These assumptions appear contradictory, but really they're not. The reason it is assumed that we want to buy while doing all sorts of other things is precisely because we don't want to devote our attention to shopping.

It's certainly true that people complain a lot about shopping. It can be extremely unpleasant. And besides, admitting you like to shop stigmatizes you, at least in some circles, as a superficial person with too much time to waste. Being overworked is, at the moment, a powerful mark of status. Nobody wants to admit to having time to shop.

People want ways of shopping that adjust to the pace of their lives. That doesn't mean that they want to spend more time adjusting to the demands of technology. Nor does it mean that they are going to stop shopping. They want the technology to help them do it.

It seems safe to predict that our attention—as shoppers, drivers, and in every other role—will continue to be divided, and that new technologies will drive us to even more elaborate distractions. One visionary idea, reported in the *Wall Street Journal,* is a new button on the car radio, which will would allow motorists to purchase any item that is being advertised, or even discussed, at any particular moment. Your momentary impulse would be fed directly to a satellite in stationary orbit above the earth, which would bounce your order to a processing center where your credit card would be charged or your bank account debited. The knowledge that the driver who just sped past you at eighty miles an hour was simultaneously choosing new draperies seems destined to be one of the terrors of the near future.

The Internet is already a great tool for doing research on individual items and their prices. It's not very useful, so far, for scanning hundreds of items at a time to find the one you want. Stores will always be better at reminding us to buy things we have forgotten, or never knew, we wanted. But computer technology that can collate and find patterns in buying decisions is increasingly able to offer new sorts of surprises.

While people may complain about shopping, they are not willing to buy things mindlessly. Shopping is a responsibility, an exercise of power. The food we eat, the clothes we wear, the objects that we have in our homes form the very basis of our lives. The choices that we make about these things play a big role in determining who we are. We don't want to surrender such power to a computer program or turn it into a game. This is a serious matter.

Most people, at least some of the time, like to shop. They don't necessarily love to shop. And they don't do it because it's lots of fun. They shop in order to feel responsible. They shop to see what other people are wearing, buying, and doing. They shop in order to discover who they are and what they might become. They shop in order to identify themselves with people they admire. They shop because they crave change. They shop to be selfish and to be generous. They shop to belong, and they shop to prevail.

Shopping is sometimes exciting, sometimes neurotic, sometimes wasteful. But it's not frivolous. We use things and give them meanings. What we're looking for—at Target, at Tiffany's, at the flea market, or on the Web—are tools and attributes, possibilities and disguises. We're looking for better times, and for rewards for our virtues that no one else will give us. We're looking for excitement, and conspire with retailers to create a benign sense of uncertainty. We're expressing our love. We're reveling in our competence. We're seeking out surprises and good prices. We hunt. We gather. We rummage. We haggle. We splurge.

We're human. And so we shop.

NOTE ON SOURCES
AND FURTHER READING

*M*ost of us retain, if only subconsciously, the prejudice that producing goods is important, masculine, and central to understanding ourselves, while consuming is trivial, feminine, and peripheral to both history and psychology. Nevertheless, since the 1970s, many anthropologist, historians, geographers, psychologists, sociologists, literary critics, specialists in women's studies, and other scholars have joined marketers in looking seriously at the expenditure side of the ledger. I have drawn on all of these disciplines to portray the development of the shopper.

This note is not a comprehensive bibliography, but rather a list, with some comments, of works that might interest those who wish to pursue further some of the topics discussed in the book.

In writing about material things, the forces that bring them into being, and the emotion they induce, it is impossible not to be influenced by Daniel Boorstin's *Americans: The Democratic Experience* (New York, 1973). James R. Beniger's *Control Revolution: Technological and Economic Origins of the Information Society* (Cambridge, Massachusetts, 1986) demonstrates that traditional distinctions between production and consumption are misleading, and that mass production wasn't truly possible without technologies to induce, predict, and control consumption. Walter Benjamin's *Arcades Project,* translated by Howard Eiland and Kevin McLaughlin, based on the German edition by Ralph Tiedemann, is a phantasmagoria of documents, notes, quotations, and impressions that provide real insight into the experience of being in Paris at the time it emerged as the world's preeminent shopping city. Richard L. Bushman's *Refinement of America: Persons, Houses, Cities* (New York, 1992) examines the emergence of American materialism as a by-product of our national ideals. Simon Schama's *Embarrassment of Riches: An Interpretation of Dutch Culture in the Golden Age* (New York, 1987) is a key work on affluence and anxiety, which was the subject of my own *Populuxe: the Look and Life of American in the 1950s and 1960s* (New York, 1986).

On the subject of shopping, Dorothy Davis's *History of Shopping* (London, 1966) is a basic text, especially for information about England. Detailed descriptions of London stores can be found in Alison Adburgham's *Shopping in Style: London from the Restoration to Edwardian Elegance* (London, 1979) and her *Shops and Shopping, 1800-1914: Where, and in What Manner the Well-Dressed Englishwoman Bought Her Clothes* (London, 1989).

The anthology *Consumption and the World of Goods,* edited by John Brewer and Roy Porter (London, 1993), contains several very useful articles on the development of the economic, technological, and psychological contexts in which shopping first emerged, including Cissie Fairchild's article "The Production and Marketing of Populuxe Goods in Eighteenth-Century Paris." Related works include *The Consumption of Culture, 1600-1800: Image, Object, Text,* edited by Ann Bermingham and John Brewer (New York, 1995); *Culture in History: Production, Consumption and Values in Historical Perspective,* edited by Joseph Melling and Jonathan Barry (Exeter, UK, 1992); *Luxury Trades and Consumerism in Ancien Régime Paris: Studies in the History of the Skilled Workforce,* edited by Robert Fox and Anthony Turner (Aldershot, UK, 1998); *Consumers and Luxury: Consumer Culture in*

Europe 1650-1850, edited by Maxine Berg and Helen Clifford (Manchester, UK, 1999); Daniel Roche, *A History of Everyday Things: The Birth of Consumption in France, 1600-1800* (New York, 2000); Neil McKendrick, *The Birth of a Consumer Society : The Commercialization of Eighteenth-Century England* (Bloomington, Indiana, 1982); Sidney W. Mintz, *Sweetness and Power: The Place of Sugar in Modern History* (New York, 1985); and S. A. M. Adshead, *Material Culture in Europe and China, 1400-1800: The Rise of Consumerism* (New York, 1997).

As is evident from the text, I am impressed by Daniel Miller's anthropological approach to contemporary shopping in different developed societies. In addition to *A Theory of Shopping* (Ithaca, New York, 1998), Miller has also written *The Dialectics of Shopping* (Chicago, 2001); and edited and contributed to the anthology *Material Cultures: Why Some Things Matter* (Chicago, 1998).

My discussion of the role of women in hunter-gatherer societies owes much to the article "Woman the Gatherer: The Role of Women in Early Hominid Evolution" by Adrienne L. Zihlman, which is included in *Reader in Gender Archaeology*, edited by Kelley Hays-Gilpin and David S. Whitley (New York, 1998). Related works include *Woman the Gatherer*, edited by Frances Dahlberg (New Haven, 1981); *Limited Wants, Unlimited Means: A Reader on Hunter-Gatherer Economics and the Environment* (Washington, 1998); and *Foragers in Context: Long-Term Regional and Historical Perspectives in Hunter-Gatherer Studies*, edited by Preston T. Miracle, Lynn E. Fisher, and Jody Brown (Ann Arbor, 1991).

There is an enormous literature drawing from several disciplines on shopping and gender. *His and Hers: Gender, Consumption, and Technology*, edited by Roger Horowitz and Arwen Mohun (Charlottesville, Virginia, 1998), offers a historically oriented selection. Others include Elizabeth Kowaleski-Wallace's *Consuming Subjects: Women, Shopping, and Business in the Eighteenth Century* (New York, 1997); Erika Diane Rappaport's *Shopping for Pleasure: Women in the Making of London's West End* (Princeton, 2000); and Hilary Radner's *Shopping Around: Feminine Culture and the Pursuit of Pleasure* (New York, 1995).

My discussion of the early markets of New York is based largely on Thomas F. De Voe's *Market Book: A History of the Public Markets of the City of New York* (New York, 1970). For ancient markets, see *Trade and Market in the Early Empires, Economies in History and Theory*, edited by Karl Polanyi, Conrad M. Arensberg, and Harry W. Pearson (Chicago, 1957); David W. Tandy, *Warriors into Traders: The Power of the Market in Early Greece* (Berkeley, California, 1997); and Joel Kaye, *Economy and Nature in the Fourteenth Century: Money, Market Exchange, and the Emergence of Scientific Thought* (New York, 1998).

For department stores, see Michael R. Miller, *The Bon Marché: Bourgeois Culture and the Department Stores, 1869-1920*, (Princeton, New Jersey, 1981); *Cathedrals of Consumption: The European Department Store, 1850-1939*, edited by Geoffrey Crossick and Serge Jaumain (Aldershot, UK, 1999); Bill Lancaster, *The Department Store: A Social History* (London, 1995); and Elaine S. Abelson, *When Ladies Go A-Thieving: Middle-Class Shoplifters in the Victorian Department Store* (New York, 1989).

On taste and design, see Adrian Forty, *Objects of Desire* (New York, 1986); Brent C. Brolin, *Flight of Fancy: The Banishment and Return of Ornament* (New York, 1985); Doreen Bolger Burke, et. al., *In Pursuit of Beauty: Americans and the Aesthetic Movement* (New York, 1987); and Wendy Kaplan, *The Art That is Life* (Boston, 1987). My discussion of the Larkin Company is based largely on Jack Quinan's *Frank Lloyd Wright's Larkin Building: Myth and Fact* (Cambridge, Massachusetts, 1987).

Valuable books on the evolution of Christmas as a consumer holiday include Mark Connelly, *Christmas: A Social History* (New York, 1999); J. M. Golby, *Making the Modern Christmas* (Athens, Georgia, 1986); Paul L. Maier, *In the Fullness of Time: A Historian Looks at Christmas, Easter, and the Early Church* (San Francisco, 1991); Stephen Nissenbaum, *The Battle for Christmas* (New York, 1996); Karal Ann Marling, *Merry Christmas! Celebrating America's Greatest Holiday* (Cambridge, Massachusetts, 2000); *Unwrapping Christmas*, edited by Daniel Miller (New York, 1993); Penne L. Restad, *Christmas in America: A History* (New York, 1995); and William Burnell

Waits, *The Modern Christmas in America: A Cultural History of Gift Giving* (New York, 1993).

Gary Cross's *All Consuming Century* (New York, 2000) is a fair-minded history that provides important insights into the commercialization of private life. Most American studies of consuming follow in the tradition of Thorstein Veblen and strike a more negative note. Among these are James B. Twitchell's *Lead Us Into Temptation: The Triumph of American Materialism* (New York, 1999); Juliet B. Schor's *Do Americans Shop Too Much?* (Boston, 2000) and *The Overworked American: The Unexpected Decline of Leisure* (New York, 1991); and Robert H. Frank's *Luxury Fever: Why Money Fails to Satisfy in an Age of Excess* (New York, 1999). For a history of thinking about consumption see Daniel Horowitz, *The Morality of Spending: Attitudes Toward the Consumer Society in America, 1875-1940* (Baltimore, 1985).

My discussion of the neurotic dimensions of shopping relies heavily on the Helen R. Woodruffe's "Compensatory Consumption: Why Women Go Shopping When They're Fed Up and Other Stories" in *Marketing Intelligence & Planning* (June–July, 1997). See also Michel Lejoyeux, et. al., "Phenomenology and Psychopathology of Uncontrolled Buying" in *America Journal of Psychiatry* (December, 1996); and the anthologies *I Shop, Therefore I Am: Compulsive Buying and the Search for Self,* edited by April Lane Benson (Northvale, New Jersey, 2000), and *Serious Shopping: Psychotherapy and Consumerism,* edited by Adrienne Baker (London, 2000).

Rachel Bowlby's *Shopping With Freud* (London, 1993) is, like the same author's *Just Looking: Consumer Culture in Dreiser, Gissing and Zola* (New York, 1985), literary criticism that highlights what fiction can tell us about attitudes toward shopping. Jane Austen's novels, especially *Persuasion,* which offers several scenes of shopping on holiday at Bath, provide a glimpse of shopping as it was becoming a woman's preoccupation. Ben Jonson's *Bartholomew Fair* (1614) provides a jaundiced view of a Puritan's mind conflicted by the temptations of the marketplace, while just about all of Shakespeare's plays deal with issues of self-creation and disguise. The title *As You Like It* seems a shopkeeper's promise, one that was perhaps familiar to a glover's son, and the comedy deals with how people fashion themselves to please others.

The most influential recent analysis of shoppers' behavior is Paco Underhill, *Why We Buy: The Science of Shopping* (New York, 1999). Underhill's methods of observing shoppers were first publicized by Malcolm Gladwell in articles for the *New Yorker*, which were adapted in his book *The Tipping Point* (Boston, 2000). David Lewis and Darren Bridger's *Soul of the New Consumer* (London, 2000) partakes of the windiness endemic to books on marketing, but it also contains useful information. There are many works that provide demographic models of marketing. I have discussed one of the most recent and most complex models, described in Michael J. Weiss, *The Clustered World: How We Live, What We Buy, and What It All Means About Who We Are* (Boston, 2000). I have also made heavy use of articles from *American Demographics* magazine, an invaluable source of information on shoppers' attitudes and acts.

B. Joseph Pine and James F. Gilmore's *Experience Economy: Work Is Theatre and Every Business a Stage* (Boston, 1999) is an enormously influential work that has convinced retailers and others that they can profit more from entertainment than from goods, while the essays in *Variations on a Theme Park*, edited by Michael Sorkin (New York, 1992), take a skeptical view of this phenomenon and its influences on our culture. Ann Satterthwaite's *Going Shopping: Consumer Choices and Community Consequences* (New Haven, 2001) is a historical survey of the impact of retailing on urban form.

There is a certain irony in that, even as Internet-based commerce was crashing and burning while I worked on this book, the Internet was becoming steadily more useful as a source of information about shopping. One can find out what is being written in newspapers and trade magazines throughout the world, and it is possible to gain access to a host of obscure and esoteric publications. Before the advent of online research, for example, I would never have thought to consult the journal *Perceptual and Motor Skills*. But because I did, I know that men walk faster on treadmills, while women walk faster in malls.

PHOTOGRAPH SOURCES

INDEX

adolescents, 144–45
advertising, 135, 196–98. *See also* marketing
aesthetic movement, 149–51
Agora market (Athens), 52–53, 190
alternative markets, 148–56, 157
Americans. *See* United States
American Wilderness Experience (AWE), 201
anonymity, 126
anti-fashion, 102–3
anxiety. *See* insecurity
Armero market (Colombia), 45–47
artisans, 69–74, 81–83, 91
arts-and-crafts movement, 151–52, 152–54, 157–58
aspirations, 134–37
Athens, 13, 51–53, 190
attention to shoppers, xvii, 113–39
  anonymity and the growth of cities and stores, 126–30
  aspirations, exclusivity, and, 134–37
  buying in quantity and, 124–25
  contemporary shoppers and, 137–39
  convenience and, 202–4, 207
  feminized buyosphere and, 119–23
  fixing prices and, 130–32
  markets and, 48
  online retail, privacy, and, 113–17
  ordeal of too much, 117–19
  ready-to-wear clothing and, 132–34
austerity, 17, 99, 152–56
authority. *See* power
automatic markdowns, 193
automobiles, 159, 195
avant-garde groups, 148–52

bargaining, 48, 206–7
bargains, 104–5, 109, 193–94, 206

barter, 54–55
Bartholomew Fair, 200–201
bazaars, 43–44, 122
belonging, xvii, 143–65
  American taste reform, 152–56
  avant-garde movements, A. L. Liberty, and, 148–52
  classifying shoppers, 161–65
  consumer behavior theories, 156–61
  fashion and, 100–103
  necessities and, 16–17
  reforming taste, 145–48
  taste and, 143–45
bibliography, 209–14
big box stores, 191
Body Shop, The, 145
Boo.com, 138–39
books, 209–14
brains, gender and, 29–31, 34
brand shopping, 195–202
Brooks, Henry Sands, 132
Brummel, Beau, 96–97
buyer profiles, 114–15
buyosphere, xiv–xv. *See also* markets; retailing; stores
  bazaar, 43–44
  early New York City and, 74–76
  self-expression and, 65–68 (*see also* self-expression)
  old-style markets, 59–62
  as women's world, 28–29, 119–23

carriage trade, 123
catalogs, mail-order, xii–xiv
celebration, xvii, 57–58, 171. *See also* Christmas
celebrity, 150–51
Centennial Exhibition of 1876, 148
Champagne fairs (France), 55–59, 69

change (coins), small, 53–55, 76
cheating, 56–57
children, 5–6, 177
China, 13, 18
choice
    evolution of, 68–69
    as freedom, 5–6, 84–85 (see also
        freedom)
    materialism and, 18–19
    as nurturing, 34–36
    responsibility and, xi
Christmas, xvii, 169–83
    development of American, 174–80
    holiday shopping, 169–72
    pre-Christmas holidays, 172–74
    Santa Claus, indulgence, and self-
        control, 180–83
    shopping for, at work, 203–4
circling, 30
cities, 68–69, 126–30, 175. See also New York
    City; Paris; Rome and Roman Empire
class, 95, 128–29, 135, 156–58
clerks. See salesclerks
clothing
    as luxury, 70, 79
    men vs. women and, 24, 28
    ready-to-wear, 132–34
    sumptuary laws and, 14, 83
    used, 79
Clustered World, The, 163
clusters, demographic, 145, 162–65
coffee and tea, 78
coins, as low-value money, 53–55
Colombia market, 45–47
communities, xiii, xvii, 43–45, 46–48,
        50–51, 153–54. See also belonging;
    families; relationships
compensatory consumption, 109
competence, 4, 23–25. See also power;
    responsibility
confidence, consumer, xv–xvi, 18–19
consumers. See also attention to shoppers;
    convenience; shopping
    children as, 5–6
    confidence of, xv–xvi, 18–19
    consumer economy, xv–xvi, 92–93
    role-relaxed, 101–3
    theories of behavior of, 156–61
convenience, xvii, 187–204
    brand shopping, 195–99
    divided attention and, 202–4
    efficiency, leisure, and, 187–90
    entertainment and, 199–202

freedom from, 36
    self-service shopping, 192–95
    types of stores and, 190–92
coupons, 39, 104, 105
courts, market, 56–57
courts, royal. See royal courts
Covent Garden, 60
Craftsman, The, 153
craftsmen, 69–74, 81–83, 91

democracy, 84, 96
demographic clusters, 145, 162–65
department stores, 105, 131–37, 148,
        191–92, 194–95
depression, 108. See also psychological
    issues
desires, xiv, xvii. See also attention to
    shoppers
De Vore, Irven, 32
discovery, xvii, 104. See also markets
displays, store, 80, 130–31
districts, shopping, 71, 80–81, 190
divided attention, 202–4, 207
dollar stores, 105, 137
Dutch West India Company, 75–76

Eastlake, Charles Locke, 151
eBay, 106–7
economizing, 39–40
efficiency, 189. See also convenience
emotional factors, 103–7, 116, 117–19,
        204. See also psychological issues
emulation, 157–58
England. See also London
    Christmas in, 174–75
    market courts, 56
    taste reform in, 147
engrossing, 56
entertainment, 27, 57, 189–90
etiquette, 98–99
Europe. See also England; France; Rome
    and Roman Empire
    coins in, 55
    early retailing in, 68–69
    fairs and markets in medieval, 45, 51,
        56–59
exclusivity, 134–37
Ezekiel, 49–50

fairs, 44–45, 55–59, 69, 200–201. See also
    markets
families, 50–51, 170, 176–78, 189–90. See
    also Christmas

far-fetched items, 71
fashion
 consciousness of, 100–103
 early, 79
 food as, 60
 insecurity and, xvii, 91, 93–96 (see also
  insecurity)
 sumptuary laws and, 14
 taste vs., 144
 in United States, 98–100
 Wedgwood china as, 96–98
fast sellers, 123–24
fear. See insecurity
feminism, 24–25, 32
Filene's, 135, 192–94
fixed prices, 131, 206
fluid prices, 206–7
food, 15–16, 52, 77–78
forestalling, 56
forks, 77
France, 81–82, 129. See also Paris
freedom
 choice as, 5–6, 84–85 (see also choice)
 identity and, 66
 insecurity vs., 92–93
future of shopping, xvi, 205–8

gatherers, women as, 31–33
gender. See men; sex; women
General Motors, 159–60
gifts
 Christmas, 175–76
 family values and, 50–51
 power and, xii–xiii, 4–5, 11–12
 wrapping, 180
Godwin, E. W., 150
gold coins, 54
Great Depression, xv, 195, 197
Great Exhibit of 1851, 147
Greece, 9–10, 13, 51–53, 190
Gresham, Sir Thomas, 72
guarantees, money-back, 136

Harrod's, 131
Hebrews, 13, 49–50
Hidden Persuaders, The, 160
hip-hop culture, 158–59
historical perspectives. See also shopping
 American Christmas, 174–80
 attention to shoppers, 117–19
 avant-garde movements, 14852
 brand shopping, 195–99
 consumer behavior theories, 156–61

 convenience, 190–92
 department stores, 134–37
 earliest shoppers, x
 feminized buyosphere, 119–23
 fixed prices, 130–32
 gifts and authority, 4–5, 11–12
 growth of stores and cities, 126–30
 holidays, 172–74
 hunter-gatherer cultures, 29, 31–34
 industrialization, 91–93, 124–25
 laws, 56–59, 81–83
 low-value money, 53–55
 luxury, 13–14
 mail-order catalogs, xii–xiv
 markets, 45–51
 materialism, 17–18, 76–81, 98–100
 New York City, 74–76
 power of objects, 4–5, 7–10
 ready-to-wear clothing, 132–34
 reforming taste, 145–48, 152–56
 self-service shopping, 192–95
 shopping districts, 68–74
 this book about, xvii
 Wedgwood china, 96–98
holiday boxes, 176
holidays, 169–74. See also Christmas
Home Depot, 27, 191
home-shopping networks, xiv, 65
Hubbard, Elbert, 153
hunter-gatherer cultures, 29, 31–34

identity, xvii, 98, 116, 144–45. See also self-
 expression
impersonal sales, 48, 61–62, 117, 136
indulgence, xi, 13, 14, 37, 172–74,
 180–83
industrialization
 Christmas and, 176
 insecurity and, 91–93
 taste and, 146
information, 46–47, 52–53
insecurity, xvii, 89–110
 development of American fashion,
  98–100
 development of Wedgwood culture,
  96–98
 fashion and, 91, 93–95
 fashion consciousness, 100–103
 fluidity and, 207
 gifts and, 12
 importance of, for shopping, 103–7
 industrialization and, 91–93
 marketing and, 89–91

shopping as sickness, 107–10
women's, 37, 120
Internet retailing
   attention to shoppers and, 113–17,
     138–39
   failure of, xv, 138–39
   future of shopping and, 205–8
   insecurity and, 105–7
   men vs. women shopping on, 28–29
   money-back guarantees, 136
   patterns of consumption and, 163
   preshopping, 100

Japan, 51, 82–83
Jesus, 54–55
Jonson, Ben, 73–74
judgment, xvii, 48, 114, 137

Kalahari Desert gatherers, 33–34, 36, 103
Kāshān bazaar, 43–44, 47–48
King of Prussia Mall, 164–65
kings. See royal courts
kleptomaniacs, 10
Kohl's, 192
Koolhaas, Rem, 150
Kris Kringle, 178
Kula valuables, 12

Larkin Manufacturing Co., 153–54
laws
   market rules, 56–57
   peace of the fair, 58–59
   restricting shopping to preserve order,
     81–83
   sumptuary, 14, 83, 84
layout, store, 133–34, 191–92
Lee, Richard, 32
leisure, xvi, 187–90, 202–4
leisure class, 156–58
Lévi-Strauss, Claude, 181
Liberty, Arthur Lazenby, 148–52
lifestyles
   demographics and, 161
   necessity and, 16–17
   taste and, 145
London. See also England
   attentiveness to shoppers in, 128–29
   brands in, 196
   buyosphere in, 67
   Covent Garden, 60
   early retailing in, 71–74, 79–81, 84
   shopping study in, 37–40
low-value money, 53–55, 76

luxury. See also materialism
   austerity as, 17
   craftsmen and, 69–74
   as decadence, 9–10, 99
   popular, 123
   textiles and, 124
   as threat to authority, 12–17

Mail-order catalogs, xii–xiv
malls
   bazaars as precursors to, 122
   clustering products, 190–91
   first, 72, 195
   outlet, 105
   as theme parks, 200
Manhattan, 76
Man the Hunter, 32
manufacturing, 81–83, 137. See also industrialization
marble palace, 122, 131, 134
markdowns, 193
marked prices, 117, 131
marketing. See also advertising
   to children, 6
   classifying contemporary shoppers,
     161–65
   gender and, 24
   insecurity and, 89–91
   packaging and, 24, 138, 197
   psychological, 159–61
   taste and, 145
   of Wedgwood china, 97 98
markets. See also buyosphere; retailing;
   stores
   Athens, 51–53
   contemporary, 59–62
   dangers of, 48–51
   evolution of, into shopping districts,
     68–74
   fairs and peace of the fair, 56–59
   low-value money and, 53–55
   scarcity and, 45–48
   sociability of, 43–45
materialism. See also luxury
   avant-garde response to, 148–52
   Christmas and, 170, 179
   dangers of markets, 49–50
   history of, 9, 17–18, 76–81, 98–100
medicine, patent, 73, 196
men. See also women
   fashion consciousness in, 100
   and shopping, 23, 24, 25–29
Meserve, Jason, 203–4

metalworking, 7–8
micromarketing, 164–65
Miller, Daniel, 37–40
mirrors, 65, 78–79
Mitchell, Arnold, 162
money
    low-value, 53–55
    new vs. old, 99
money-back guarantees, 136
Moore, Clement W., 176
moral issues, x–xi, 48–49, 171–72
Morris, William, 151
mourning, 124–25
museums, 147–48

necessity and needs, xii–xiv, 12–17. *See also* luxury
Netherlands, 74–77
new money, 99
New Year's Day, 175
New York City
    buyosphere in, 67, 74–76
    Union Square, 53, 59–60
    World Trade Center attacks, 18–19, 49–50, 170
niche markets, 153
Niketown, 199–200
Nine American Lifestyles, The, 162
nobles. *See also* royal courts
nonreciprocal acquisition, 9. *See also* stealing
novelty, 67
nurturing, xvii, 34–36. *See also* responsibility

objects, x, 4–5, 144
obligations, 11–12, 24
old money, 99
online retailing. *See* Internet retailing
outlet malls, 105. *See also* malls

packaging, 24, 138, 197
Packard, Vance, 160
palpeuse shoppers, 129–30
Paris, 71, 81–82, 126–28, 129–30, 131, 134. *See also* France
patent medicine, 73, 196
Patten, Simon, 17–18
peace of the fair, 58–59
personal sales, 47–48, 60–61
Philadelphia, 59–60, 61–62
pie powder courts, 56–57
Pike Place, 53, 60

polling, 161
power, xvi, 3–19
    cities and, 69–70
    gifts and, 11–12
    insecurity vs., 92–93
    luxury vs. necessity and, 12–17
    materialism and, 17–19
    objects and, 4–5, 7–10
    responsibility and, 24 (*see also* responsibility)
    restricting shopping to preserve, 81–83
    shopping as, 3–4, 5–6
preshopping, 100
Priceline.com, 205–6
prices
    fixed, 117, 206
    marked, 117, 131
    online comparison of, 105–6
    Woolworth's, 137
Prince Albert, 125, 147–48, 179
privacy, 17, 115–16
problem shoppers, 107–10
productivity, 203–4
product packaging, 24, 138, 197
profiles, buyer, 114–15
psychological issues
    children as consumers, 5–6
    consumer confidence, xv–xvi
    emotion, 103–7, 116, 117–19, 204
    marketing and, 159–61
    novelty, 67
    retailing and, 136–37
    shoplifting, 10
    shopping as sickness, 18, 92, 107–10
Puritans, 9, 175

radio advertising, 197–98
Reading Terminal Market, 59
ready-to-wear clothing, 132–34
Real Simple, 155
references, 209–14
relationships, ix–x. *See also* communities; families
    Christmas and, 170
    gifts and, 11–12
    insecurity vs., 92–93
    markets and, 46–48, 50–51
    women and, 31
religion
    coins and, 54–55
    fairs and, 57–58
    materialism and, 13, 49–50
    religious objects, 8

Santa Claus and, 181 (*see also* Christmas)
shopping as sacrifice, 38–40
Renfrew, Colin, 7–8
research, market, 160–61. *See also* marketing
responsibility, xvii, 23–40. *See also* women
choice and, xi
choosing as nurturing, 34–36
future of shopping and, 208
hierarchy of creation and, 68
holidays and release from, 171
reasons for differences between women and men, 29–34
shopping as escape from, 109–10
shopping as ritual of sacrifice, 37–40
women and, 23–25
women vs. men as shoppers, 25–29
retailing. *See also* buyosphere; markets; stores
beginnings of, 68–74
Christmas, 182–83
low-value money and, 54
Internet (*see* Internet retailing)
salesclerks (*see* salesclerks)
self-service, 192–95
wholesaling and, 56
retail therapy, 109
role-relaxed consumers, 101–3
Rome and Roman Empire, 13–14, 45, 51, 54–55, 172, 196
royal courts
power of objects, 8–9
restrictions of shopping by, 81–83
taste and, 146
Royal Exchange, 72
Roycrofters, 153
rules. *See* laws

sacredness. *See* religion
sacrifice, 38–40, 173–74
saints, fairs and, 57–58
salesclerks. *See also* attention to shoppers
anxiety about, 121
brand shopping and, 195–96
changing roles of, 131, 135–36, 137, 193
quality of service of, 138–39
Santa Claus, 180–81
scarcity, xvii. *See also* insecurity
automatic markdowns and, 193
fashion and, 91, 93–96
markets and, 45–48
Scott, Walter Dill, 160

Seattle, 53, 60
self-control, 180–83
self-expression, xvii, 65–85
buyosphere and, 65–68 (*see also* buyosphere)
choice as freedom, 84–85
development of retail trade, 68–74
early New York retailing, 74–76
explosion of belongings, 76–81
insecurity vs., 92–93
restricting shopping to preserve order, 81–83
self-respect, 102–3
self-service shoppers, 192–95, 198
service, 138–39. *See also* salesclerks
sex, ix–x, 108, 121–22, 129. *See also* men; women
Shakespeare, 74, 94
shell currency, 76
Shirky, Clay, 206
shirts, 24
shopaholics, 107–10
shoplifting, 10
shoppers. *See* consumers
shopping
attention, desires, and, xvii (*see also* attention to shoppers)
belonging, taste, and, xiii, xvii (*see also* belonging)
buyosphere and, xiv–xv (*see also* buyosphere)
celebration, Christmas, and, xvii (*see also* Christmas)
convenience and, xvii (*see also* convenience)
discovery and, xvii (*see also* markets)
future of, 205–8
gifts and, xii–xiii (*see also* gifts)
history of, x, xvii (*see also* historical perspectives)
insecurity and, xvii (*see also* fashion; insecurity)
power and, x, xvi (*see also* power)
responsibility, women, and, x–xi, xvii (*see also* responsibility; women)
self-expression and, xvii (*see also* self-expression)
sex, relationships, and, ix–x
this book about, xvi–xvii
why people shop, ix–xvi
shops, 70–71, 122–23. *See also* stores
shoputainment, 200
sickness, shopping as, 107–10

silver coins, 54, 55
simplicity, 17, 99, 152–56
sociability, markets and, 43–45, 46–48
sociological issues, 161–65
sources, bibliographic, 209–14
sport-utility vehicles, 14
stability, political, 48–49, 54–55
standards, market, 56–57, 198
status, 46, 156–58. *See also* class
stealing, 9–10, 79
Stewart, A. T., 122, 131, 134
Stewart, Martha, 154
Stickley, Gustav, 153
sticky Web sites, 107
stores. *See also* buyosphere; markets;
    retailing
  clusters of, 80–81
  convenience and types of, 190–92
  growth of, 126–30, 133–34
  layout of, 134, 191–92
  shops, 70–71, 122–23
strangers, xvii, 50, 57. *See also* markets
strip centers, 191, 194
suburbanization, 194
sumptuary laws, 14, 83, 84. *See also* laws
superfluity, 17–18
supermarkets, 35–36, 61, 65, 104–5, 194, 198
surpluses, 44, 50–51

tailoring, 132–33
taste, xvii, 143–48. *See also* belonging
television, xiv, 197–98
textile industry, 91–92, 123–25, 131–32. *See also* clothing
theme parks, retailing and, 200
Theory of Shopping, A, 38
Theory of the Leisure Class, The, 156
thrift, 39–40
time, saving, 189, 198. *See also* convenience
Toronto, 60
transformation, xii–xiii
tree, Christmas, 179
Trobriand Islands, 12
trust, 54–55
Tyre, 49

umbrellas, 82
uncertainty principle, 104–5. *See also* insecurity
Union Square, 53, 59–60
United States
  attentiveness to shoppers in, 129–30

development of Christmas in, 174–80
development of fashion in, 98–100
markets in, 59–62
men vs. women as shoppers, 23
New York City (*see* New York City)
rise of women as shoppers, 120
simplicity and taste reform in, 148, 152–56
World Trade Center attacks, 18–19, 49–50, 170
urban centers. *See* cities

vacation shopping, 201–2
vacuum cleaner, shopping for, 25–27
VALS (values and lifestyles) model, 162
value, fashion vs., 102–3
values, 50–51
Veblen, Thorstein, 156–58, 202
Victoria and Albert Museum, 147
"Visit from Saint Nicholas, A," 176

Wal-Mart, 3–4, 15, 16, 18–19, 45, 137–38
Walton, Sam, 138
Wanamaker, John, 134, 135, 136, 179, 192
wastefulness, xi, 18, 37, 157
wealth, 24, 50–51
Web. *See* Internet retailing
WebHouse, 205–6
Wedgwood, Josiah, 96–98
Wedgwood china, 89–91, 95–98
Weiss, Michael, 163
Whitely, William, 128–29
wholesaling, 52, 56. *See also* retailing
Wilde, Oscar, 149
windows, 65, 80, 119
women
  Christmas and, 176–78
  fashion conscious, 100
  feminized buyosphere and, 119–23
  men vs., as shoppers, 24, 25–34
  as problem shoppers, 107–8
  and responsibility, 23–25, 193 (*see also* responsibility)
  shopping as nurturing, 34–36
  shopping as sacrifice, 37–40
  Wedgwood china and, 97
Woodruffe, Helen R., 109
Woolworth, Frank W., 137
work, shopping and, 202–4
workshops, 70–71
World Trade Center attacks, 19, 49–50, 170
wrapping, gift, 180